A Delicate Balance

Date: 4/24/17

812.54 ALB
Albee, Edward, 1928-
A delicate balance :a play /

BY EDWARD ALBEE

The Zoo Story
The Death of Bessie Smith
The Sandbox
The American Dream
Who's Afraid of Virginia Woolf?
The Ballad of the Sad Cafe
Tiny Alice
Malcolm
A Delicate Balance
Everything in the Garden
Box and Quotations from Chairman Mao Tse-Tung
All Over
Seascape
Listening
Counting the Ways
The Lady from Dubuque
Lolita
The Man Who Had Three Arms
Finding the Sun
Marriage Play
Three Tall Women
Fragments (A Sit-Around)
The Play About the Baby
The Goat or, Who is Sylvia?
Occupant
At Home at the Zoo
Me, Myself & I

A Delicate Balance

A PLAY

EDWARD ALBEE

OVERLOOK DUCKWORTH
New York • London

For John Steinbeck
Affection and admiration

INTRODUCTION

A DELICATE BALANCE

—A Non-reconsideration

My mind is going, I suspect; I have no idea how long I've known most of my friends; the names of most people are beyond me, and I cannot recall the emotional or physical experience of the writing of most of my plays, or how long ago the experience I cannot recall occurred.

The only senses I fully retain—and very sharply these—are picture images and sounds. Hearing two bars of almost any piece of serious music has me naming the composer, the piece, and often the date of composition and opus number—or K., or Hoboken, or whatever. Seeing a painting for a second time—in a new context, of course—has me instantly recalling on what wall it hung, in what room, in what country, when I saw it first.

But names and events . . . that's another matter. Once I looked straight at my mother and couldn't figure out who she was. (Well, I guess we've all had that one!)

So . . . is it *really* thirty years since the first production of *A Delicate Balance*? It seems like yesterday, as they say? No, certainly not . . . but thirty years?

The play has not changed; that *I* can see. I've had to rewrite only two lines—making it clear that topless bathing suits (for women, of course) are not made anymore, and changing "our dear Republicans as dull as ever" to "as brutal as ever" (that second change long overdue).

The play does not seem to have "dated"; rather, its points seem clearer now to more people than they were in its lovely first production. Now, in its lovely new production (I will not say "revival"; the thing was not dead—unseen, unheard perhaps, but lurking), it seems to me exactly the same experience. No time has passed; the characters have not aged or become strange. (The upper-upper middle-class WASP culture has *always* been just a little bizarre, of course.)

The play concerns—as it always has, in spite of early-on critical misunderstanding—the rigidity and ultimate paralysis which afflicts those who settle in too easily, waking up one day to discover that all the choices they have avoided no longer give them any freedom of choice, and that what choices they do have left are beside the point.

I have become odder with time, I suppose (my next play but one will be about a goat, for God's sake), but *A Delicate Balance,* bless it, does not seem to have changed much—aged nicely, perhaps. Could we all say the same.

—Edward Albee
Montauk, N.Y.
August 1996

A *Delicate Balance* opened in New York City on September 12, 1966, at the Martin Beck Theatre.

JESSICA TANDY *as* AGNES

HUME CRONYN *as* TOBIAS

ROSEMARY MURPHY *as* CLAIRE

CARMEN MATHEWS *as* EDNA

HENDERSON FORSYTHE *as* HARRY

MARIAN SELDES *as* JULIA

Directed by ALAN SCHNEIDER

The Lincoln Center Theatre production of *A Delicate Balance* opened in New York City on April 21, 1996, at the Plymouth Theatre.

ROSEMARY HARRIS *as* AGNES

GEORGE GRIZZARD *as* TOBIAS

ELAINE STRITCH *as* CLAIRE

ELIZABETH WILSON *as* EDNA

JOHN CARTER *as* HARRY

MARY BETH HURT *as* JULIA

Directed by GERALD GUTIERREZ

CHARACTERS

AGNES
A handsome woman in her late 50's

TOBIAS
Her husband, a few years older

CLAIRE
Agnes' sister, several years younger

JULIA
Agnes' and Tobias' daughter 36, angular

EDNA AND HARRY
Very much like Agnes and Tobias

THE SCENE

*The living room of a large and well-appointed suburban house.
Now.*

ACT ONE

(*In the library-living room.* AGNES *in a chair,* TOBIAS *at a shelf, looking into cordial bottles*)

AGNES

(*Speaks usually softly, with a tiny hint of a smile on her face: not sardonic, not sad . . . wistful, maybe*)

What I find most astonishing—aside from that belief of mine, which never ceases to surprise me by the very fact of its surprising lack of unpleasantness, the belief that I might very easily—as they say—lose my mind one day, not that I suspect I am about to, or am even . . . nearby . . .

TOBIAS

(*He speaks somewhat the same way*)

There is no saner woman on earth, Agnes.

(*Putters at the bottles*)

AGNES

. . . for I'm not that sort; merely that it is not beyond . . . happening: some gentle loosening of the moorings sending the balloon adrift—and I think that is the only outweighing thing: adrift; the . . . becoming a stranger in . . . the world, quite . . . uninvolved, for I never see it as violent, only a drifting—what are you looking for, Tobias?

TOBIAS

We will all go mad before you. The anisette.

AGNES (*A small happy laugh*)

Thank you, darling. But I could never do it—go adrift—for what would become of you? Still, what I find most astonishing, aside, as I said, from that speculation—and I wonder, too, sometimes, if I am the only one of you to admit to it: not that *I* may go mad, but that each of you wonders if each of *you* might not—why on earth do you want anisette?

TOBIAS *(Considers)*

I thought it might be nice.

AGNES *(Wrinkles her nose)*

Sticky. I will do cognac. It is supposed to be healthy—the speculation, or the assumption, I suppose, that if it occurs to you that you might be, then you are not; but I've never been much comforted by it; it follows, to my mind, that since I speculate I might, some day, or early evening I think more likely—some autumn dusk—go quite mad, then I very well might.

(Bright laugh)

Some autumn dusk: Tobias at his desk, looks up from all those awful bills, and sees his Agnes, mad as a hatter, chewing the ribbons on her dress . . .

TOBIAS *(Pouring)*

Cognac?

AGNES

Yes; Agnes Sit-by-the-fire, her mouth full of ribbons, her mind aloft, adrift; nothing to do with the poor old thing but put her in a bin some-where, sell the house, move to Tucson, say, and pine in the good sun, and live to be a hundred and four.

(He gives her her cognac)

Thank you, darling.

TOBIAS *(Kisses her forehead)*

Cognac is sticky, too.

AGNES

Yes, but it's nicer. Sit by me, hm?

TOBIAS *(Does so; raises his glass)*

To my mad lady, ribbons dangling.

AGNES *(Smiles)*

And, of course, I haven't worn the ribbon dress since Julia's remarriage. Are you comfortable?

TOBIAS

For a little.

AGNES

What astonishes me most—aside from my theoretically healthy fear—no, not fear, how silly of me—healthy speculation that I might some day become an embarrassment to you . . . what I find most astonishing in this world, and with all my years . . . is Claire.

TOBIAS *(Curious)*

Claire? Why?

AGNES

That anyone—be they one's sister, or not—can be so . . . well, I don't want to use an unkind word, 'cause we're cozy here, aren't we?

TOBIAS *(Smiled warning)*

Maybe.

AGNES

As the saying has it, the one thing sharper than a serpent's tooth is a sister's ingratitude.

TOBIAS

(Getting up, moving to a chair)
The saying does not have it that way.

AGNES

Should. Why are you moving?

TOBIAS

It's getting uncomfortable.

AGNES *(Semi-serious razzing)*

Things get hot, move off, huh? Yes?

TOBIAS *(Not rising to it)*

I'm not as young as either of us once was.

AGNES *(Toasting him)*

I'm as young as the day I married you—though I'm certain I don't look it—because you're a very good husband . . . most of the time. But I was talking about Claire, or was beginning to.

TOBIAS

(Knowing shaking of the head)
Yes, you were.

AGNES

If I were to list the mountain of my burdens—if I had a thick pad and a month to spare—that bending my shoulders *most*, with the possible exception of Julia's trouble with marriage, would be your—it must be instinctive, I think, or *reflex*, that's more like it—your reflex defense of everything that Claire . . .

TOBIAS
(Very nice, but there is steel underneath)
Stop it, Agnes.

AGNES *(A little laugh)*
Are you going to throw something at me? Your glass? My goodness, I
hope not . . . that awful anisette all over everything.

TOBIAS *(Patient)*
No.

AGNES *(Quietly daring him)*
What then?

TOBIAS *(Looking at his hand)*
I shall sit very quietly . . .

AGNES
. . . as always . . .

TOBIAS
. . . yes, and I shall will you to apologize to your sister for what I must in
truth tell you I thought a most . . .

AGNES
Apologize! To her? To Claire? I have spent my adult life apologizing *for*
her; I will not double my humiliation by apologizing *to* her.

TOBIAS *(Mocking an epigram)*
One does not apologize to those for whom one must?

AGNES *(Winking slowly)*
Neat.

TOBIAS
Succinct, but one of the rules of an aphorism . . .

AGNES
An epigram, I thought.

TOBIAS *(Small smile)*
An epigram is usually satiric, and you . . .

AGNES
. . . and I am grimly serious. Yes?

TOBIAS
I fear so.

AGNES

To revert specifically from Claire to . . . her effect, what *would* you do were I to . . . spill my marbles?

TOBIAS *(Shrugs)*

Put you in a bin somewhere, sell the house and move to Tucson. Pine in the hot sun and live forever.

AGNES *(Ponders it)*

Hmmm, I bet you would.

TOBIAS *(Friendly)*

Hurry, though.

AGNES

Oh, I'll *try*. It won't be simple paranoia, though, I know that. I've tried so hard, to . . . well, you know how little I vary; goodness, I can't even raise my voice except in the most calamitous of events, and I find that both joy and sorrow work their . . . wonders on me more . . . evenly, slowly, wit*hin*, than most: a suntan rather than a scalding. There are no mountains in my life . . . nor chasms. It is a rolling, pleasant land . . . verdant, my darling, thank you.

TOBIAS *(Cutting a cigar)*

We do what we can.

AGNES *(Little laugh)*

Our motto. If we should ever go downhill, have a crest made, join things, we must have that put in Latin—We do what we can—on your blazers, over the mantel; maybe we could do it on the linen, as well . . .

TOBIAS

Do you think I should go to Claire's room?

AGNES *(Silence: then stony, firm)*

No.

*(*TOBIAS *shrugs, lights his cigar)*

Either she will be down, or not.

TOBIAS

We do what we can?

AGNES

Of course.

(Silence)

So, it will not be simple paranoia. Schizophrenia, on the other hand, is

far more likely—even given the unlikelihood. I believe it can be chemi-
cally induced . . .

(*Smiles*)

if all else should fail; if sanity, such as it is, should become too much.
There are times when I think it would be so . . . proper, if one could take
a pill—or even inject—just . . . remove.

TOBIAS (*Fairly dry*)

You should take drugs, my dear.

AGNES

Ah, but those are temporary; even addiction is a repeated temporary . . .
stilling. I am concerned with peace . . . not mere relief. And I am not a
compulsive—like . . . like some . . . like our dear Claire, say.

TOBIAS

Be kind. Please?

AGNES

I think I should want to have it fully . . . even on the chance I could not
. . . come back. Wouldn't that be terrible, though? To have done it,
induced, if naturally looked unlikely and the hope was there?

(*Wonder in her voice*)

Not be able to come back? Why did you put my cognac in the tiny glass?

TOBIAS (*Rising, going to her*)

Oh . . . I'm sorry. . . .

AGNES

(*Holding her glass out to him; he takes it from her*)

I'm not a sipper tonight; I'm a breather: my nose buried in the glass, all
the wonder there, and very silent.

TOBIAS

(*Getting her a new cognac*)

I thought Claire was much better tonight. I didn't see any need for you
to give her such a going-over.

AGNES (*Weary*)

Claire was *not* better tonight. Honestly, Tobias!

TOBIAS

(*Clinging to his conviction*)

I thought she was.

AGNES *(Putting an end to it)*

Well, she was *not.*

TOBIAS

Still . . .

AGNES

(Taking her new drink)

Thank you. I have decided, all things considered, that I shall not induce, that all the years we have put up with each other's wiles and crotchets have earned us each other's company. And I promise you as well that I shall think good thoughts—healthy ones, positive—to ward off madness, should it come by . . . uninvited.

TOBIAS *(Smiles)*

You mean I have no hope of Tucson?

AGNES

None.

TOBIAS *(Mock sadness)*

Hélas . . .

AGNES

You have hope, only, of growing even older than you are in the company of your steady wife, your alcoholic sister-in-law and occasional visits . . . from our melancholy Julia.

(A little sad)

That is what you have, my dear Tobias. Will it do?

TOBIAS

(A little sad, too, but warmth)

It will do.

AGNES *(Happy)*

I've never doubted that it would.

(Hears something, says sourly)

Hark.

(CLAIRE has entered)

Did I hear someone?

TOBIAS

(Sees CLAIRE standing, uncomfortably, away from them)

Ah, there you are. I said to Agnes just a moment ago . . .

CLAIRE

(To AGNES' *back, a rehearsed speech, gone through but hated)*
I must apologize, Agnes; I'm . . . very sorry.

AGNES

(Not looking at her; mock surprise)
But what are you sorry *for,* Claire?

CLAIRE

I apologize that my nature is such to bring out in you the full force of
your brutality.

TOBIAS *(To placate)*
Look, now, I think we can do without any of this sort of . . .

AGNES

(Rises from her chair, proceeds toward exiting)
If you come to the dinner table unsteady, *if* when you try to say good
evening and weren't the autumn colors lovely today you are nothing but
vowels, and *if* one smells the vodka on you from across the room—and
don't tell me again, *either* of you! that vodka leaves nothing on the breath:
if you are expecting it, if you are sadly and wearily expecting it, it *does*—
if these conditions exist . . . *persist* . . . then the reaction of one who is burdened by her love is not brutality—though it would be excused, believe
me!—not brutality at all, but the souring side of love. If I scold, it is
because I wish I needn't. If I am sharp, it is because I am neither less nor
more than human, and if I am to be accused once again of making too
much of things, let me remind you that it is my manner and not the matter. I apologize for being articulate. Tobias, I'm going to call Julia, I think.
Is it one or two hours' difference? . . . I can never recall.

TOBIAS *(Dry)*
Three.

AGNES

Ah, yes. Well, be kind to Claire, dear. She is . . . injured.
(Exits. A brief silence)

TOBIAS

Ah, well.

CLAIRE

I have never known whether to applaud or cry. Or, rather, I never know
which would be the more appreciated—expected.

TOBIAS *(Rather sadly)*

You are a great damn fool.

CLAIRE *(Sadly)*

Yes. Why is she calling Julia?

TOBIAS

Do you want a quick brandy before she comes back?

CLAIRE *(Laughs some)*

Not at all; a public one. Fill the balloon half up, and I shall sip it ladylike, and when she . . . glides back in, I shall lie on the floor and balance the glass on my forehead. That will give her occasion for another paragraph, and your ineffectual stop-it-now's.

TOBIAS

(Pouring her brandy)

You *are* a great damn fool.

CLAIRE

Is Julia having another divorce?

TOBIAS

Hell, I don't know.

CLAIRE *(Takes the glass)*

It's only your daughter. Thank you. I should imagine—from all that I have . . . watched, that it is come-home time.

(Offhand)

Why don't you kill Agnes?

TOBIAS *(Very offhand)*

Oh, no, I couldn't do that.

CLAIRE

Better still, why don't you wait till Julia separates and comes back here, all sullen and confused, and take a gun and blow all our heads off? . . . Agnes first—through respect, of course, then poor Julia, and finally—if you have the kindness for it—me?

TOBIAS *(Kind, triste)*

Do you really want me to shoot you?

CLAIRE

I want you to shoot Agnes first. Then I'll think about it.

TOBIAS

But it would have to be an act of passion—out of my head, and all that.
I doubt I'd stand around with the gun smoking, Julia locked in her room
screaming, wait for you to decide if you wanted it or not.

CLAIRE

But unless you kill Agnes . . . how will I ever know whether I want to live?
  (*Incredulous*)
An act of passion!?

TOBIAS (*Rather hurt*)

Well . . . yes.

CLAIRE (*Laughs*)

Oh, my; *that's* funny.

TOBIAS (*Same*)

I'm sorry.

CLAIRE (*Friendly laugh*)

Oh, my darling Tobias, *I'm* sorry, but I just don't see you in the role, that's
all—outraged, maddened into action, proceeding by reflex . . . Can you
see yourself, though? In front of the judge? Predictable, stolid Tobias?
"It all went blank, your honor. One moment, there I was, deep in my
chair, drinking my . . ." What is that?

TOBIAS

Anisette.

CLAIRE

"Anisette." Really? Anisette?

TOBIAS (*Slightly edgy*)

I *like* it.

CLAIRE (*Wrinkles her nose*)

Sticky. "There I was, your honor, one moment in my chair, sipping at
my anisette . . . and the next thing I knew . . . they were all lying about,
different rooms, heads blown off, the gun still in my hand. I . . . I have no
recollection of it, sir." Can you imagine that, Tobias?

TOBIAS

Of course, with all of you dead, your brains lying around in the rugs,
there'd be no one to say it *wasn't* an act of passion.

CLAIRE

Leave me till last. A breeze might rise and stir the ashes. . . .

TOBIAS

Who's that?

CLAIRE

No one, I think. Just sounds like it should be.

TOBIAS

Why don't you go back to your . . . thing . . . to your alcoholics thing?

CLAIRE *(Half serious)*

Because I don't like the people. . . .

TOBIAS

What is it called?

CLAIRE

Anonymous.

TOBIAS

Yes; that. Why don't you go back?

CLAIRE *(Suddenly rather ugly)*

Why don't you mind your own hooting business?

TOBIAS *(Offended)*

I'm sorry, Claire.

CLAIRE *(Kisses at him)*

Because.

TOBIAS

It was better.

CLAIRE

(Holds her glass out; he hesitates)

Be a good brother-in-law; it's only the first I'm not supposed to have.

TOBIAS *(Pouring for her)*

I thought it was better.

CLAIRE

Thank you.

(Lies on the floor, balances glass on her forehead, puts it beside her, etc.)

You mean Agnes thought it was better.

TOBIAS *(Kindly, calmly)*

No, I thought so too. That it would be.

CLAIRE

I told you: not our type; nothing in common with them. When you used to go to business—before you became a squire, parading around the ancestoral manse in jodhpurs, confusing the gardener . . .

TOBIAS *(Hurt)*

I've never done any such thing.

CLAIRE

Before all that . . .
  (Smiles, chuckles)
sweet Tobias. . . when you used to spend all your time in town . . . with your business friends, your indistinguishable if not necessarily similar friends . . . what did you have in common with them?

TOBIAS

Well, uh . . . well, everything.
  (Maybe slightly on the defensive, but more . . . vague)
Our business; we all mixed well, were friends away from the office, too . . . clubs, our . . . an, an environment, I guess.

CLAIRE

Unh-huh. But what did you have in common with them? Even Harry: your very best friend . . . in all the world—as far as you know; I mean, you haven't met everybody . . . are you switching from anisette?

TOBIAS *(Pouring himself brandy)*

Doesn't go for a long time. All right?

CLAIRE

Doesn't matter to *me.* Your very best friend . . . Tell me, dear Tobias; what do you have in common with him? Hm?

TOBIAS *(Softly)*

Please, Claire . . .

CLAIRE

What do you really have in common with your very best friend . . . 'cept the coincidence of having cheated on your wives in the same summer with the same woman . . . girl . . . woman? What except that? And hardly a distinction. I believe she was upended that whole July.

TOBIAS *(Rather tight-mouthed)*

If you'll forgive me, Claire, common practice is hardly . . .

CLAIRE

Poor girl, poor whatever-she-was that hot and very *wet* July.

(Hard)

The distinction would have been to have not: to have been the one or two of the very, very many and oh, God, similar who did not upend the poor . . . unfamiliar thing that dry and oh, so wet July.

TOBIAS

Please! Agnes!

CLAIRE *(Quieter)*

Of course, you had the wanton only once, while Harry! Good friend Harry, I have it from the horse's mouth, was on top for good and keeps twice, with a third try not so hot in the gardener's shed, with the mulch, or whatever it is, and the orange pots . . .

TOBIAS *(Quietly)*

Shut your mouth.

CLAIRE

(Stands, faces TOBIAS; softly)

All right.

(Down again)

What was her name?

TOBIAS *(A little sad)*

I don't remember.

CLAIRE *(Shrugs)*

No matter; she's gone.

(Brighter)

Would you give friend Harry the shirt off your back, as they say?

TOBIAS

(Relieved to be on something else)

I *suppose* I would. He *is* my best friend.

CLAIRE *(Nicely)*

How sad does that make you?

TOBIAS

(Looks at her for a moment, then)

Not much; some; not much.

CLAIRE

No one to listen to Bruckner with you; no one to tell you're sick of golf; no one to admit to that—now and then—you're suddenly frightened and you don't know why?

TOBIAS *(Mild surprise)*

Frightened? No.

CLAIRE *(Pause; smile)*

All right. Would you like to know what happened last time I climbed the stairs to the fancy alkie club, and why I've not gone back? What I have *not* in common with those people?

TOBIAS *(Not too enthusiastic)*

Sure.

CLAIRE *(Chuckle)*

Poor Tobias. "Sure." Light me a cigarette?

(TOBIAS hesitates a moment, then lights her one)

That will give me everything.

(He hands the lighted cigarette to her; she is still on the floor)

I need. A smoke, a sip and a good hard surface. Thank you.

(Laughs a bit at that)

TOBIAS *(Standing over her)*

Comfy?

CLAIRE

(Raises her two arms, one with the cigarette, the other the brandy glass; it is a casual invitation. TOBIAS looks at her for a moment, moves a little away)

Very. Do you remember the spring I moved out, the time I was *really* sick with the stuff: was drinking like the famous fish? Was a source of great embarrassment? So that you and Agnes set me up in the apartment near the station, and Agnes was *so* good about coming to see me?

(TOBIAS sighs heavily)

Sorry.

TOBIAS *(Pleading a little)*

When will it all . . . just go in the past . . . forget itself?

CLAIRE

When all the defeats are done, admitted. When memory takes over and corrects fact . . . makes it tolerable. When Agnes lies on her deathbed.

TOBIAS

Do you know that Agnes has . . . such wonderful control I haven't seen her cry in . . . for the longest time . . . no matter what?

CLAIRE

Warn me when she's coming; I'll act drunk. Pretend you're very sick, Tobias, like you were with the stomach business, but pretend you feel your insides are all green, and stink, and mixed up, and your eyes hurt and you're half deaf and your brain keeps turning off, and you've got peripheral neuritis and you can hardly walk and you hate. You hate with the same green stinking sickness you feel your bowels have turned into . . . yourself, and *everybody*. Hate, and, oh, God!! you want love, l-o-v-e, so badly—comfort and snuggling is what you really mean, of course—but you hate, and you notice—with a sort of detachment that amuses you, you think—that you're more like an animal every day . . . you snarl, and *grab* for things, and hide things and forget where you hid them like not-very-bright dogs, and you wash less, prefer to *be* washed, and once or twice you've actually soiled your bed and laid in it because you can't get up . . . pretend all that. No, you don't like that, Tobias?

TOBIAS

I don't know why you want to . . .

CLAIRE

You want to know what it's like to be an alkie, don't you, boy?

TOBIAS *(Sad)*

Sure.

CLAIRE

Pretend all that. So the guy you're spending your bottles with starts you going to the old A.A. And, you sit there at the alkie club and watch the . . . better ones—not recovered, for once an alkie, always, and you'd better remember it, or you're gone the first time you pass a saloon—you watch the better ones get up and tell their stories.

TOBIAS *(Wistful, triste)*

Once you drop . . . you can come back up part way . . . but never . . . really back again. Always . . . descent.

CLAIRE

(Gently, to a child)
Well, that's life, baby.

TOBIAS

You are a great, damn fool.

CLAIRE

But, I'm not an alcoholic. I am not now and never was.

TOBIAS *(Shaking his head)*

All the promise . . . all the chance . . .

CLAIRE

It would be so much simpler if I *were*. An alcoholic.
(She will rise and re-enact during this)
So, one night, one month, sometime, I'd had one martini—as a Test to see if I could—which, given my . . . stunning self-discipline, had become three, and I felt . . . rather daring and nicely detached and a little bigger than life and not snarling yet. So I marched, more or less straight, straight up to the front of the room, hall, and faced my peers. And I looked them over—all of them, trying so hard, grit and guilt and failing and trying again and loss . . . and I had a moment's—sweeping—pity and disgust, and I almost cried, but I didn't—like sister like sister, by God—and I heard myself say, in my little-girl voice—and there were a lot of different me's by then—"I am a alcoholic."
(Little-girl voice)
"My name is Claire, and I am a alcoholic."
(Directly to TOBIAS)
You try it.

TOBIAS

(Rather vague, but not babytalk)
My name is . . . My name is Claire, and I am an alcoholic.

CLAIRE

A alcoholic.

TOBIAS *(Vaguer)*

A alcoholic.

CLAIRE

"My name is Claire, and I am a . . . alcoholic." Now, I was supposed to go on, *you* know, say how bad I was, and didn't want to be, and How It Happened, and What I Wanted To Happen, and Would They Help Me Help Myself . . . but I just stood there for a . . . ten seconds maybe, and then I curtsied; I made my little-girl curtsy, and on my little-girl feet I padded back to my chair.

TOBIAS

(After a pause; embarrassedly)
Did they laugh at you?

CLAIRE

Well, an agnostic in the holy of holies doesn't get much camaraderie, a little patronizing, maybe. Oh, they were taken by the *vaude*ville, don't misunderstand me. But the one lady was nice. She came up to me later and said, "You've taken the first step, dear."

TOBIAS *(Hopeful)*

That was nice of her.

CLAIRE *(Amused)*

She didn't say the first step toward *what,* of course. Sanity, *in*sanity, revelation, self-deception. . . .

TOBIAS *(Not much help)*

Change . . . sometimes . . . no matter what . . .

CLAIRE *(Cheerful laugh)*

Count on you, Tobias . . . snappy phrase every time. But it *hooked* me— the applause, the stage presence . . . that beginning; no school tot had more gold stars for never missing class. I went; oh, God, I *did.*

TOBIAS

But stopped.

CLAIRE

Until I learned . . .

(AGNES enters, unobserved by either TOBIAS or CLAIRE)

. . . and being a slow student then in my young middle-age, slowly . . . that I was not, nor had ever been . . . a alcoholic . . . or an. Either. What I did not have in common with those people. That they were alcoholics, and I was not. That I was just a drunk. That they couldn't help it; I could, and wouldn't. That they were sick, and I was merely . . . willful.

AGNES

I have talked to Julia.

TOBIAS

Ah! How is she?

AGNES *(Walking by CLAIRE)*

My, what an odd glass to put a soft drink in. Tobias, you have a quiet sense of humor, after all.

TOBIAS

Now, Agnes . . .

CLAIRE

He has not!

AGNES *(Rather heavy-handed)*
Well, it *can't* be brandy; Tobias is a grown-up, and knows far better than to . . .

CLAIRE
(Harsh, waving her glass)
A toast to you, sweet sister; I drink your—not health; persistence—in good, hard brandy, *âge inconnu.*

AGNES
(Quiet, tight smile, ignoring CLAIRE*)*
It *would* serve you right, my dear Tobias, were I to go away, drift off. You would not have a woman left about you—only Claire and Julia . . . not even people; it would serve you right.

CLAIRE *(Great mocking)*
But I'm not an alcoholic, baby!

TOBIAS
She . . . she can drink . . . a little.

AGNES
(There is true passion here; we see under the calm a little)
I WILL NOT TOLERATE IT!! I WILL NOT HAVE YOU!
(Softer but tight-lipped)
Oh, God. I wouldn't mind for a moment if you filled your bathtub with it, lowered yourself in it, DROWNED! I rather wish you would. It would give me the peace of mind to know you could do something well, thoroughly. If you want to kill yourself—then do it *right!*

TOBIAS

Please, Agnes . . .

AGNES
What I cannot stand is the selfishness! Those of you who want to die . . . and take your whole lives doing it.

CLAIRE
(Lazy, but with loathing under it)
Your wife is a perfectionist; they are *very* difficult to live with, these people.

TOBIAS
(To AGNES, *a little pleading in it)*
She isn't an alcoholic . . . she says; she can drink some.

CLAIRE
(Little-child statement, but not babytalk)
I am not a alcoholic!

AGNES
We think that's very nice. We shall all rest easier to know that it is willful; that the vomit and the tears, the muddy mind, the falls and the absences, the cigarettes out on the tabletops, the calls from the club to come and get you please . . . that they are all . . . willful, that it *can* be helped.
(Scathing but softly)
If you are not an alcoholic, you are beyond forgiveness.

CLAIRE *(Ibid.)*
Well, I've been that for a long time, haven't I, sweetheart?

AGNES
(Not looking at either of them)
If we change for the worse with drink, we are an alcoholic. It is as simple as that.

CLAIRE
And who is to say!

AGNES
I!

CLAIRE *(A litany)*
If we are to live here, on Tobias' charity, then we are subject to the will of his wife. If we were asked, at our father's dying . . .

AGNES *(Final)*
Those are the ground rules.

CLAIRE *(A sad smile)*
Tobias?
(Pause)

Nothing?

(*Pause*)

Are those the ground rules? Nothing? Too . . . settled? Too . . . dried up? Gone?

(*Nicely*)

All right.

(*Back to* AGNES)

Very well, then, Agnes, you win. I shall be an alcoholic.

(*The smile too sweet*)

What are you going to do about it?

AGNES

(*Regards* CLAIRE *for a moment, then decides she*—CLAIRE—*is not in the room with them.* AGNES *will ignore* CLAIRE's *coming comments until otherwise indicated.* TOBIAS *will do this, too, but uncomfortably, embarrassedly*)

Tobias, you will be unhappy to know it, I suppose, or of mixed emotions, certainly, but Julia is coming home.

CLAIRE (*A brief laugh*)

Naturally.

TOBIAS

Yes?

AGNES

She is leaving Douglas, which is no surprise to *me*.

TOBIAS

But, wasn't Julia happy? You didn't tell me anything about . . .

AGNES

If Julia were happy, she would not be coming home. *I* don't want her here, God knows. I mean she's welcome, of course . . .

CLAIRE

Right on schedule, once every three years . . .

AGNES

(*Closes her eyes for a moment, to keep ignoring* CLAIRE)

. . . it *is* her home, we are her parents, the *two* of us, and we have our obligations to her, and I have reached an age, Tobias, when I wish we were always alone, you and I, without . . . hangers-on . . . or anyone.

CLAIRE *(Cheerful but firm)*

Well, I'm not going.

AGNES

. . . but if she and Doug are through—and I'm not suggesting *she* is in the right—then her place is properly here, as for some it is not.

CLAIRE

One, two, three, four, down they go.

TOBIAS

Well, I'd like to talk to Doug.

AGNES

(As if the opposite answer were expected from her)
I wish you would! If you had talked to Tom, or Charlie, yes! even Charlie, or . . . uh . . .

CLAIRE

Phil?

AGNES

(No recognition of CLAIRE *helping her)*
. . . Phil, it might have done some good. If you've decided to assert yourself, finally, too late, I imagine . . .

CLAIRE

Damned if you do, damned if you don't.

AGNES

. . . Julia might, at the very least, come to think her father cares, and that might be consolation—if not help.

TOBIAS

I'll . . . I'll talk to Doug.

CLAIRE

Why don't you invite him *here?* And while you're at it, bring the others along.

AGNES *(Some reproach)*
And you might talk to Julia, too. You don't, very much.

TOBIAS

Yes.

CLAIRE *(A mocking sing-song)*
Philip loved to gamble.
Charlie loved the boys,
Tom went after women,
Douglas . . .

AGNES *(Turning on* CLAIRE*)*
Will you stop that?

CLAIRE
Ooh, I *am* here, after all. I exist!

AGNES
Why don't you go off on a vacation, Claire, now that Julia's coming home again? Why don't you go to Kentucky, or Tennessee, and visit the distilleries? Or why don't you lock yourself in your room, or find yourself a bar with an apartment in the back. . . .

CLAIRE
Or! Agnes; why don't you die?
*(*AGNES *and* CLAIRE *lock eyes, stay still)*

TOBIAS
(Not rising from his chair, talks more or less to himself)
If I saw some point to it, I might—if I saw some reason, chance. If I thought I might . . . break through to her, and say, "Julia . . . ," but then what would I say? "Julia . . ." Then, nothing.

AGNES
(Breaking eye contact with CLAIRE, *says, not looking at either)*
If we do not love someone . . . never have loved them . . .

TOBIAS *(Soft correction)*
No; there can be silence, even having.

AGNES
(More curious than anything)
Do you really want me dead, Claire?

CLAIRE
Wish, yes. Want? I don't know; probably, though I might regret it if I had it.

AGNES
Remember the serpent's tooth, Tobias.

TOBIAS *(Recollection)*

The cat that I had.

AGNES

Hm?

TOBIAS

The cat that I had . . . when I was—well, a year or so before I *met* you. She was very old; I'd had her since I was a kid; she must have been seventeen, or more. An alley cat. She didn't like people very much, I think; when people came . . . she'd . . . pick up and walk away. She liked *me;* or, rather, when I was alone with her I could see she was content; she'd sit on my lap. I don't know if she was happy, but she was content.

AGNES

Yes.

TOBIAS

And how the thing happened I don't really know. She . . . one day she . . . well, one day I realized she no longer liked me. No, that's not right; one day I realized she must have stopped liking me some time before. One evening I was alone, home, and I was suddenly aware of her absence, not just that she wasn't in the room with me, but that she hadn't been, in rooms with me, watching me shave . . . just *about* . . . for . . . and I couldn't place *how* long. She hadn't gone *away,* you understand; well, she *had,* but she hadn't run off. I knew she was *around;* I remembered I had caught sight of her—from time to time—under a chair, moving out of a room, but it was only when I realized something had happened that I could give any pattern to things that had . . . that I'd noticed. She didn't like me any more. It was that simple.

CLAIRE

Well, she was old.

TOBIAS

No, it wasn't that. She didn't like me any more. I tried to force myself on her.

AGNES

Whatever do you mean?

TOBIAS

I'd close her in a room with me; I'd pick her up, and I'd *make* her sit in my lap; I'd make her stay there when she didn't want to. But it didn't work; she'd abide it, but she'd get down when she could, go away.

CLAIRE

Maybe she was ill.

TOBIAS

No, she wasn't; I had her to the vet. She didn't like me anymore. One night—I was *fixed* on it now—I had her in the room with me, and on my lap for the . . . the what, the fifth time the same evening, and she lay there, with her back to me, and she wouldn't purr, and I *knew:* I knew she was just waiting till she could get down, and I said, "Damn you, you like me; God damn it, you stop this! I haven't *done* anything to you." And I shook her; I had my hands around her shoulders, and I shook her . . . and she bit me; hard; and she hissed at me. And so I hit her. With my open hand, I hit her, smack, right across the head. I . . . I *hated* her!

AGNES

Did you hurt her badly?

TOBIAS

Yes; well, not badly; she . . . I must have hurt her ear some; she shook her head a lot for a day or so. And . . . you see, there was no *reason.* She and I had lived together and been, well, you know, friends, and . . . there was no *reason.* And I hated her for that. I hated her, well, I suppose because I was being accused of something, of . . . failing. But, I hadn't been cruel, by design; if I'd been neglectful, well, my life was . . . I resented it. I resented having a . . . being judged. Being *betrayed.*

CLAIRE

What did you do?

TOBIAS

I had *lived* with her; I had done . . . *everything.* And . . . and if there was a, any responsibility I'd failed in . . . well . . . there was nothing I could *do.* And, and I was being accused.

CLAIRE

Yes; what did you do?

TOBIAS

(*Defiance and self-loathing*)
I had her killed.

AGNES (*Kindly correcting*)
You had her put to sleep. She was old. You had her put to sleep.

TOBIAS *(Correcting)*

I had her killed. I took her to the vet and he took her . . . he took her into the back and

(Louder)

he gave her an injection and killed her! I had her *killed!*

AGNES *(After a pause)*

Well, what else could you have done? There was nothing to be done; there was no . . . meeting between you.

TOBIAS

I might have tried longer. I might have gone on, as long as cats live, the same way. I might have worn a hair shirt, locked myself in the house with her, done penance. For *something.* For *what.* God knows.

CLAIRE

You probably did the right *thing* Distasteful alternatives; the less . . . ugly choice.

TOBIAS

Was it?

(A silence from them all)

AGNES *(Noticing the window)*

Was that a car in the drive?

TOBIAS

"If we do not love someone . . . never have loved someone . . ."

CLAIRE *(An abrupt, brief laugh)*

Oh, stop it! "Love" is not the problem. You love Agnes and Agnes loves Julia and Julia loves me and I love you. We all love each other; yes we do. We love each other.

TOBIAS

Yes?

CLAIRE *(Something of a sneer)*

Yes; to the depths of our self-pity and our greed. What else but love?

TOBIAS

Error?

CLAIRE *(Laughs)*

Quite possibly: love and error.

(There is a knock at the door; AGNES *answers it)*

AGNES

Edna? Harry? What a surprise! Tobias, it's Harry and Edna. Come in.
Why don't you take off your . . .

(HARRY *and* EDNA *enter. They seem somewhat ill at ease, strained
for such close friends*)

TOBIAS

Edna!

EDNA

Hello, Tobias.

HARRY

(*Rubbing his hands; attempt at being bluff*)
Well, now!

TOBIAS

Harry!

CLAIRE (*Too much surprise*)

Edna!
(*Imitates* HARRY's *gruff voice*)
Hello, there, Harry!

EDNA

Hello, dear Claire!
(*A little timid*)
Hello, Agnes.

HARRY (*Somewhat distant*)

Evening. . . Claire.

AGNES

(*Jumping in, just as a tiny silence commences*)
Sit *down*. We were just having a cordial. . . .
(*Curiously loud*)
Have you been . . . out? Uh, to the club?

HARRY

(*Is he ignoring* AGNES' *question?*)
I like this room.

AGNES

To the club?

CLAIRE

(Exaggerated, but not unkind)

How's the old Harry?

HARRY *(Self-pity entering)*

Pretty well, Claire, not as good as I'd like, but . . .

EDNA

Harry's been having his shortness of breath again.

HARRY *(Generally)*

I can't breathe sometimes . . . for just a bit.

TOBIAS *(Joining them all)*

Well, two sets of tennis, you know.

EDNA

(As if she can't remember something)

What have you done to the room, Agnes?

AGNES

(Looks around with a little apprehension, then relief)

Oh, the summer *things* are off.

EDNA

Of course.

AGNES

(Persisting in it, a strained smile)

Have you been to the club?

HARRY *(To TOBIAS)*

I was talking to Edna, 'bout having our books done in leather; bound.

TOBIAS

Oh? Yes?

(Brief silence)

CLAIRE

The question—'less I'm going deaf from all the alcohol—was

(Southern accent)

"Have you-all been to the club?"

AGNES

(Nervous, apologetic covering)

I wondered!

HARRY *(Hesitant)*

Why . . . no, no.

EDNA *(Ibid.)*

Why, why, no, Agnes. . . .

AGNES

I wondered, for I thought perhaps you'd dropped by here on your way
from there.

HARRY

. . . no, no . . .

AGNES

. . . or perhaps that we were having a party, and I'd lost a day. . . .

HARRY

No, we were . . . just sitting home.

EDNA *(Some condolence)*

Agnes.

HARRY *(Looking at his hands)*

Just . . . sitting home.

AGNES

(Cheerful, but lack of anything better to say)
Well.

TOBIAS

Glad you're here! Party or not!

HARRY *(Relieved)*

Good to see you, Tobias!

EDNA *(All smiles)*

How is Julia?!

CLAIRE

Wrong question.
   (Lifts her glass)
May I have some brandy, Tobias?

AGNES

(A savage look to CLAIRE, *back to* EDNA*)*
She's coming home . . . I'm afraid.

EDNA *(Disappointment)*

Oh . . . not again!

TOBIAS

(Getting CLAIRE's *glass, attempted levity)*
Just can't keep that one married, I guess.

EDNA

Oh, Agnes, what a shame!

HARRY

(More embarrassed than sorry)
Gee, that's too bad.
  (Silence)

CLAIRE

Why *did* you come?

AGNES

Please! Claire!
  (Back, reassuring)
We're *glad* you're here; we're glad you came to surprise us!

TOBIAS *(Quickly)*

Yes!
  *(*HARRY *and* EDNA *exchange glances)*

HARRY

(Quite sad and curious about it)
We were . . . sitting home . . . just sitting home. . . .

EDNA

Yes . . .

AGNES *(Mildly reproving)*
We're *glad* to *see* you.

CLAIRE *(Eyes narrowing)*
What happened, Harry?

AGNES *(Sharp)*

Claire! Please!

TOBIAS

(Wincing a little, shaking his head)
Claire . . .

EDNA *(Reassuring him)*

It's all right, Tobias.

AGNES

I don't see why people have to be questioned when they've come for a friendly . . .

CLAIRE *(Small victory)*

Harry wants to tell you, Sis.

EDNA

Harry?

HARRY

We . . . well, we were sitting home . . .

TOBIAS

Can I get you a drink, Harry?

HARRY *(Shakes his head)*

. . . I . . . we thought about going to the club, but . . . it's, it's so crowded on a Friday night . . .

EDNA *(Small voice, helpful, quiet)*

. . . with the canasta party, and getting ready for the dance tomorrow . . .

HARRY

. . . we didn't want to do that, and I've . . . been tired, and we didn't want to do that . . .

EDNA

. . . Harry's been tired this whole week.

HARRY

. . . so we had dinner home, and thought we'd stay . . .

EDNA

. . . rest.

HARRY

So we were sitting, and Edna was doing that—that panel she works on . . .

EDNA *(Wistful, some loss)*

. . . my needlepoint . . .

HARRY

. . . and I was reading my French; I've got it pretty good now—not the
accent, but the . . . the words.

(A brief silence)

CLAIRE (Quietly)

And then?

HARRY

(Looks over to her, a little dreamlike, as if he didn't know where
he was)

Hmm?

CLAIRE (Nicely)

And then?

HARRY (Looks at EDNA)

I . . . I don't know quite what happened then; we . . . we were . . . it was
all very quiet, and we were all alone . . .
(EDNA begins to weep, quietly; AGNES notices, the others do not;
AGNES does nothing)
. . . and then . . . nothing happened, but . . .
(EDNA is crying more openly now)
. . . nothing at all happened, but . . .

EDNA (Open weeping; loud)

WE GOT . . . FRIGHTENED.
(Open sobbing; no one moves)

HARRY (Quiet wonder, confusion)

We got scared.

EDNA (Through her sobbing)

WE WERE . . . FRIGHTENED.

HARRY

There was nothing . . . but we were very scared.
(AGNES comforts EDNA, who is in free sobbing anguish. CLAIRE
lies slowly back on the floor)

EDNA

We . . . were . . . terrified.

HARRY

We were scared.

(Silence; AGNES *comforting* EDNA. HARRY *stock still. Quite inno-*
cent, almost childlike)
It was like being lost: very young again, with the dark, and lost. There
was no . . . thing . . . to be . . . frightened of, but . . .

EDNA *(Tears, quiet hysteria)*
WE WERE FRIGHTENED . . . AND THERE WAS NOTHING.
(Silence in the room)

HARRY
(Matter-of fact, but a hint of daring under it)
We couldn't stay there, and so we came here. You're our very best friends.

EDNA *(Crying softly now)*
In the whole world.

AGNES
(Comforting, arms around her)
Now, now, Edna.

HARRY *(Apologizing some)*
We couldn't go anywhere else, so we came here.

AGNES *(A deep breath, control)*
Well, we'll . . . you did the right thing . . . of course.

TOBIAS
Sure.

EDNA
Can I go to bed now? Please?

AGNES
(Pause; then, not quite understanding)
Bed?

HARRY
We can't go back there.

EDNA
Please?

AGNES *(Distant)*
Bed?

EDNA

I'm so . . . tired.

HARRY

You're our best friends in the world. Tobias?

TOBIAS

(A little bewilderment; rote)
Of course we are, Harry.

EDNA *(On her feet, moving)*

Please?
(Cries a little again)

AGNES

(A million things going through her head, seeping through management)
Of . . . of course you can. There's . . . there's Julia's room, and . . .
(Arm around EDNA)
Come with me, dear.
(Reaches doorway; turns to TOBIAS; a question that has no answer)
Tobias?

HARRY

(Rises, begins to follow EDNA, rather automaton-like)
Edna?

TOBIAS *(Confused)*

Harry?

HARRY *(Shaking his head)*

There was no one else we could go to.
(Exits after AGNES and EDNA. CLAIRE sits up, watches TOBIAS, as he stands for a moment, looking at the floor: silence)

CLAIRE *(A small, sad chuckle)*

I was wondering when it would begin . . . when it would start.

TOBIAS

(Hearing her only after a moment)
Start?
(Louder)

START?
(Pause)
WHAT?!

CLAIRE *(Raises her glass to him)*
Don't you know yet?
(Small chuckle)
You will.

CURTAIN

ACT TWO

SCENE ONE

(Same set; before dinner, next evening JULIA *and* AGNES *alone.* AGNES *sitting,* JULIA *on her feet, pacing maybe)*

JULIA
(Anger and self-pity; too loud)
Do you think I like it? Do you?

AGNES *(No pleading)*
Julia! Please!

JULIA
DO YOU!? Do you think I enjoy it?

AGNES
Julia!

JULIA
Do you think it gives me some kind of . . . martyr's pleasure? Do you?

AGNES
Will you be still?

JULIA
WELL!?

AGNES
THERE IS A HOUSE FULL OF PEOPLE!

JULIA
Yes! What *about* that! I come home: my room is full of Harry and Edna. I have no place to put my things. . . .

AGNES *(Placating)*
They'll go to Tobias' room, he'll sleep with me. . . .

JULIA *(Muttered)*
That'll be different.

AGNES
What did you say, young lady?

JULIA
I SAID, THAT WILL BE NICE.

AGNES
You did *not* say any such thing. You said . . .

JULIA
What are they *doing* here? Don't they have a house anymore? Has the market gone bust without my knowing it? I may have been out of touch, but . . .

AGNES
Just . . . let it be.

JULIA
(Between her teeth; controlled hysteria)
Why are they here?

AGNES
(Weary; head back; calm)
They're . . . frightened. Haven't you heard of it?

JULIA *(Incredulous)*
They're . . . what!?

AGNES *(Keeping her voice down)*
They're frightened. Now, will you let it be!

JULIA *(Offended)*
What are they frightened of? Harry and *Edna?* Frightened?

AGNES
I don't . . . I don't know yet.

JULIA
Well, haven't you *talked* to them about it? I mean, for God's sake. . . .

AGNES *(Trying to stay calm)*
No. I haven't.

JULIA
What have they done: stayed up in their room all day—*my* room!—not come down? Locked in?

AGNES

Yes.

JULIA

Yes what?

AGNES

Yes, they have stayed up in their room all day.

JULIA

My room.

AGNES

Your room. Now, let it be.

JULIA

(Almost goes on in the same tone; doesn't; very nice, now)

No, I . . .

AGNES

Please?

JULIA

I'm sorry, Mother, sorry for screeching.

AGNES

I am too old—as I remember—to remember what it is like to be a daughter, if my poor parents, in their separate heavens, will forgive me, but I am sure it is simpler than being a mother.

JULIA *(Slight edge)*

I said I was sorry.

AGNES

(All of this more for her own bemusement and amusement than anything else)

I don't recall if I ever asked my poor mother that. I do wish sometimes that I had been born a man.

JULIA

(Shakes her head; very matter-of-fact)

Not so hot.

AGNES

Their concerns are so simple: money and death—making ends meet until they meet the end.

(Great self-mockery and exaggeration)

If they *knew* what it was like . . . to be a wife; a mother; a lover; a home-maker; a nurse; a hostess, an agitator, a pacifier, a truth-teller, a deceiver . . .

JULIA
(Saws away at an invisible violin; sings)
Da-da-dee; da-da-da.

AGNES *(Laughs softly)*
There is a book out, I believe, a new one by one of the thirty million psy-chiatrists practicing in this land of ours, a book which opines that the sexes are reversing, or coming to resemble each other too much, at any rate. It is a book to be read and disbelieved, for it disturbs our sense of well-being. If the book is right, and I suspect it is, then I would be no better off as a man . . . would I?

JULIA
(Sober, though tongue-in-cheek agreement; shaking of head)
No. Not at all.

AGNES *(Exaggerated fret)*
Oh! There is nowhere to rest the weary head . . . or whatever.
(Hand out; loving, though a little grand)
How are you, my darling?

JULIA *(A little abrupt)*
What?

AGNES
(Hand still out; somewhat strained)
How are you, my darling?

JULIA *(Gathering energy)*
How is your darling? Well, I was trying to tell you before you shut me up with Harry and Edna hiding upstairs, and . . .

AGNES
ALL RIGHT!
(Pause)

JULIA *(Strained control)*
I will try to tell you, Mother—once again—before you've turned into a man. . . .

AGNES

I shall try to hear you out, but if I feel my voice changing, in the middle of your . . . rant, you will have to forgive my male prerogative, if I become uncomfortable, look at my watch, or jiggle the change in my pocket . . .

(Sees JULIA *marching toward the archway as* TOBIAS *enters*)

. . . where do you think you're going?

JULIA (*Head down, muttered*)

. . . you go straight to hell . . .

TOBIAS (*Attempt at cheer*)

Now, now, what's going on here?

JULIA

(*Right in front of him; force*)

Will you shut her up?

TOBIAS (*Overwhelmed*)

Will I . . . what?

AGNES

(*Marching toward the archway herself*)

Well, there you are, Julia; your father may safely leave the room now, I think.

(*Kisses* TOBIAS *on the cheek*)

Hello, my darling.

(*Back to* JULIA)

Your mother has arrived. Talk to *him!*

(*To* TOBIAS)

Your daughter is in need of consolation or a great cuffing around the ears. I don't know which to recommend.

TOBIAS (*Confused*)

Have . . . have Harry and Edna . . . ?

AGNES (*Exiting*)

No, they have not.

(*Gone*)

TOBIAS (*After her, vaguely*)

Well, I thought maybe . . .

(*To* JULIA, *rather timid*)

What was that . . . all about?

JULIA

As they say: I haven't the faintest.

TOBIAS (*Willing to let it go*)

Oh.

JULIA (*Rather brittle*)

Papers?

TOBIAS

Oh, yes; want them?

JULIA

Anything happy?

TOBIAS (*Hopefully*)

My daughter's home.

JULIA (*Not giving in*)

Any other joys?

TOBIAS

Sorry.
 (*Sighs*)
No; small wars, large anxieties, our dear Republicans as brutal as ever, a teen-age marijuana nest not far from here. . . .
 (*Some wonder*)
I've never had marijuana . . . in my entire life.

JULIA

Want some?

TOBIAS

Wasn't fashionable.

JULIA

What the hell do Harry and Edna want?

TOBIAS (*Scratches his head*)

Just let it be.

JULIA

Didn't you try to talk to them today? I mean . . .

TOBIAS

(*Not embarrassed, but not comfortable either*)
Well, no; they weren't down when I went off to the club, and . . .

JULIA

Good old golf?

TOBIAS (*Surprisingly nasty*)

Don't ride me, Julia, I warn you.

JULIA (*Nervously nicer*)

I've never had any marijuana, either. Aren't I a good old girl?

TOBIAS

(*Thinking of something else*)

Either that or lying.

JULIA

(*Exploding; but anger, not hysteria*)

Great Christ! What the hell did I come home to? And why? Both of you? Snotty, mean . . .

TOBIAS

LOOK!

(*Silence; softer, but no nonsense*)

There are some . . . times, when it all gathers up . . . too much.

JULIA (*Nervously*)

Sure, sure.

TOBIAS (*Not put off*)

Some *times* when it's going to be Agnes and Tobias, and not just Mother and Dad. Right? Some *times* when the allowances aren't going to be made. What are you doing, biting off your fingernails now?

JULIA (*Not giving in*)

It broke off.

TOBIAS

There are some *times* when it's all . . . too much. *I* don't know what the hell Harry and Edna are doing sitting up in that bedroom! Claire is drinking, she and Agnes are at each other like a couple of . . . of . . .

JULIA (*Softly*)

Sisters?

TOBIAS

What? The goddamn government's at me over some deductions, and you!

JULIA *(Head high, defiant)*

And me? Yes?

TOBIAS

This isn't the first time, you know. This isn't the first time you've come back with one of your goddamned marriages on the rocks. Four! Count 'em!

JULIA *(Rage)*

I know how many marriages I've gotten myself into, you . . .

TOBIAS

Four! You expect to come back here, nestle in to being fifteen and misunderstood each time!? You are thirty-six years old, for God's sake! . . .

JULIA

And you are one hundred! Easily!

TOBIAS

Thirty-six! Each time! Dragging your . . . your—I was going to say pride—your marriage with you like some Raggedy Ann doll, by the foot. You, you fill this house with your whining. . . .

JULIA *(Rage)*

I DON'T ASK TO COME BACK HERE!!

TOBIAS

YOU BELONG HERE!

(Heavy breathing from both of them, finally a little rueful giggle; TOBIAS *speaks rather nonchalantly now)*

Well. Now that I've taken out on my only daughter the . . . disgust of my declining years, I'll mix a very good and very strong martini. Join me?

JULIA *(Rather wistful)*

When I was a very little girl—well, when I was a little girl: after I'd gotten over my two year burn at suddenly having a brother, may his soul rest, when I was still a little girl, I thought you were a marvel—saint, sage, daddy, everything. And then, as the years turned and I reached my . . . somewhat angular adolescence . . .

TOBIAS

(At the sideboard; unconcerned)

Five to one? Or more?

JULIA

And then, as the years turned—poor old man—you sank to cipher, and you've stayed there, I'm afraid—very nice but ineffectual, essential, but not-really-thought-of, gray . . . noneminence.

TOBIAS (*Mixing hardly listening*)

Unh-hunh . . .

JULIA

And now you've changed again, sea monster, ram! Nasty, violent, absolutely human man! Yes, as you make it, five to one, or better.

TOBIAS

I made it about seven, I think.

JULIA

Your transformations amaze me. How can I have changed so much? Or *is* it really you?

(*He hands her a drink*)

Thank you.

TOBIAS (*As they both settle*)

I told Agnes that I'd speak to Doug . . . if you think that would do any good. By golly, Dad, that's a good martini!

JULIA

Do you really want to talk to Doug? You won't get anywhere: the compulsives you can get somewhere with—or the illusion of getting—the gamblers, the fags, the lechers . . .

TOBIAS

. . . of this world . . .

JULIA

. . . yes, you can have the illusion 'cause they're after something, the jackpot, somehow: break the bank, find the boy, climb the babe . . . something.

TOBIAS

You do pick 'em.

JULIA (*Pregnant*)

Do I?

TOBIAS

Hm?

JULIA

Do I pick 'em? I thought it was fifteen hundred and six, or so, where daughter went with whatever man her parents thought would hold the fief together best, or something. "Love will come after."

TOBIAS *(Grudging)*

Well, you may have been pushed on Charlie. . . .

JULIA

Poor Charlie.

TOBIAS *(Temper rising a little)*

Well, for Christ's sake, if you miss him so much . . .

JULIA

I do not miss him! Well, yes, I do, but not that way. Because he seemed so like what Teddy would have been.

TOBIAS

(Quiet anger and sorrow)

Your brother would not have grown up to be a fag.

JULIA *(Bitter smile)*

Who is to say?

TOBIAS *(Hard look)*

I!

(Pause. CLAIRE *in the archway)*

CLAIRE

Do I breathe gin?

*(*JULIA *sees her, runs to her, arms out, both of them, they envelop each other)*

Darling!

JULIA

Oh, my sweet Claire!

CLAIRE

Julia Julia.

JULIA

(Semi-mock condemnation)

I must say the welcome-home committee was pretty skimpy, you and Daddy gone. . . .

CLAIRE

Oh, now.

(*To* TOBIAS)

I said, do I breathe gin?

TOBIAS (*Not rising*)

You do.

CLAIRE (*Appraising* JULIA)

Well, you don't look too bad for a quadruple amputee, I must say. Are you going to make me a whatever, Tobias?

(*To* JULIA)

Besides, my darling, it's getting to be rather a habit, isn't it?

JULIA (*False smile*)

Yes, I suppose so.

CLAIRE

(*Sees* TOBIAS *is not moving*)

Then I shall make my own.

TOBIAS (*Getting up; wearily*)

Sit down, Claire, I'll do it.

CLAIRE

I wouldn't want to tax you, now.

(*Generally*)

Well, I had an adventure today. Went into town, thought I'd shake 'em up a little, so I tried to find me a topless bathing suit.

JULIA (*Giggling*)

You didn't!

TOBIAS

(*At the sideboard, disapproving*)

Really, Claire.

CLAIRE

Yes, I did.

JULIA

They're not making them anymore.

CLAIRE

I know. Shhhh. I went into what's-their-names', and I went straight up to the swimwear, as they call it, department and I got me an eighteen-nineties schoolteacher type, who wondered what she could do for me,

(JULIA *giggles*)

and I felt like telling her, "Not much, sweetheart" . . .

TOBIAS

Are you sure you wouldn't rather have a . . .

CLAIRE

Very. But I said, "Hello, there, I'm in the market for a topless swimsuit." Hurry up there, Toby. "A what, Miss?" she said, which I didn't know whether to take as a compliment or not. "A topless swimsuit," I said. "I don't know what you mean," she said after a beat. "Oh, certainly you do," I said, "no top, stops at the waist, latest thing, lots of freedom." "Oh, yes," she said, looking at me like she was seeing the local madam for the first time, "those." Then a real sniff. "I'm afraid we don't carry . . . those." "Well, in that case," I told her, "do you have any separates?" "Those we carry," she said, "those we do." And she started going under the counter, and I said, "I'll just buy the bottoms of one of those."

JULIA

No! You didn't!

CLAIRE

Yes, I did. She came up from under the counter, adjusted her spectacles and said, "What did you say?"

TOBIAS

Shall I bring it, or will you come for it?

CLAIRE

You bring. I said, "I said, 'I'll buy the bottom of one of those.'" She thought for a minute, and then she said, with ice in her voice, "And what will we do with the tops?" "Well," I said, "why don't you save 'em? Maybe bottomless swimsuits'll be in *next* year."

(JULIA *laughs openly*)

Then the poor sweet thing gave me a look I couldn't tell was either a D minus, or she was going to send me home with a letter to my mother, and she said, sort of far away, "I think you need the manager." And off she walked.

TOBIAS

(*Handing* CLAIRE *her martini; mildly amused throughout*)

What were you doing buying a bathing suit in October, anyway?

JULIA

Oh, Dad!

CLAIRE

No, now; it's a man's question.

(*Sips*)

Wow, what a good martini.

TOBIAS

(*Still standing over her, rather severe*)

Truth will get you nowhere. Why?

CLAIRE

Why? Well.

(*Thinks*)

. . . maybe I'll go on a trip somewhere.

TOBIAS

That would please Agnes.

CLAIRE (*Nods*)

As few things would. What I meant was, maybe Toby'll walk in one day, trailing travel folders, rip his tie off, announce he's fed up to there with the north, the east, the suburbs, the regulated great gray life, dwindling before him—poor Toby—and has bought him an island off Paraguay . . .

TOBIAS

. . . which has no seacoast . . .

CLAIRE

. . . yes, *way* off—has bought him this island, and is taking us all to *that*, to hack through the whatever, build us an enormous lean-to, all of us. Take us away, to where it is always good and happy.

(*Watches* TOBIAS, *who looks at his drink, frowning a little*)

JULIA (*She, too*)

Would you, Dad?

TOBIAS

(*Looks up, sees them both looking at him, frowns more*)

It's . . . it's too late, or something.

(*Small silence*)

CLAIRE *(To lighten it)*

Or, maybe I simply wanted a topless bathing suit.

(Pause)

No? Well, then . . . maybe it's more complicated yet. I mean, Claire couldn't find herself a man if she tried, and here comes Julia, home from the wars . . .

TOBIAS *(Quiet contradiction)*

You could find a man.

CLAIRE *(Some bitterness)*

Indeed, I have found several, briefly, and none my own.

TOBIAS

(To JULIA; *terribly offhand)*

Julia, don't you think Auntie Claire could find herself a man?

JULIA *(Didactic)*

I *don't* like the subject.

CLAIRE

. . . and here comes Julia, home from the wars, four purple hearts . . .

JULIA

Why don't you just have another drink and stop it, Claire?

CLAIRE

(Looks at her empty glass, shrugs)

All right.

JULIA *(Rather defensive)*

I have *left* Doug. We are not *divorced.*

CLAIRE

Yet! Are you cooking a second batch, Tobias?

(Back to JULIA)

But you've come back home, haven't you? And didn't you—with the others?

JULIA *(Her back up)*

Where else am I supposed to go?

CLAIRE

It's a great big world, baby. There are hotels, new cities. Home is the quickest road to Reno I know of.

JULIA *(Condescending)*

You've had a lot of experience in these matters, Claire.

CLAIRE

Sidelines! Good seats, right on the fifty-yard line, objective observer.

(Texas accent, or near it)

I swar! Ef I din't love muh sister so, Ah'd say she got yuh hitched fur the pleasure uh gettin' yuh back.

JULIA	TOBIAS
ALL RIGHT!	THAT WILL DO NOW!

CLAIRE

(In the silence that follows)

Sorry. Very . . . very sorry.

(AGNES appears through the archway)

AGNES

(What she may have overheard she gives no indication of)

"They" tell me in the kitchen . . . "they" tell me we are about to dine. In a bit. Are we having a cocktail? I think one might be nice.

(Puts her arm around JULIA as she passes her)

It's one of those days when everything's underneath. But, we are all together . . . which is something.

JULIA

Quite a few of us.

TOBIAS

Any word from . . .

(Points to the ceiling)

. . . up there?

AGNES

No. I dropped upstairs—well, *that* doesn't make very much sense, does it?—I *happened* upstairs, and I knocked at Harry and Edna's *Julia's* room, door, and after a moment I heard Harry say, "It's all right; we're all right." I didn't have the . . . well, I felt such an odd mixture of . . . embarrassment and irritation, and . . . apprehension, I suppose, and . . . fatigue . . . I didn't persevere.

TOBIAS

Well, haven't they been *out?* I mean, haven't they eaten or anything?

AGNES

Will you make me a . . . thing, a martini, please? I am told—*"they"* tell
me that while we were all out, at our various whatever-they-may-be's,
Edna descended, asked them to make sandwiches, which were brought
to the closed door and handed in.

TOBIAS

Well, God, I mean . . .

AGNES *(Rather a recitation)*

There is no point in pressing it, they are our very dear friends, they will
tell us in good time.

CLAIRE

(Looking through her glass)
I had a glimmer of it last night; thought I knew.

AGNES *(So gracious)*

That which we see in the bottom of our glass is most often dregs.

CLAIRE

(Peers into her glass, over-curious)
Really? Truly so?

TOBIAS

(Holding a glass out to AGNES*)*
Did you say you wanted?

AGNES

(Her eyes still on CLAIRE*)*
Yes, I did, thank you.

CLAIRE

I have been trying, without very much success, to find out why Miss Julie
here is come home.

AGNES

I would imagine Julia is home because she wishes to be, and it is where
she belongs if she wants.

TOBIAS

That's logistics, isn't it?

AGNES

You too?

JULIA

He's against everything!

AGNES

Your father?

JULIA

Doug!

AGNES

You needn't make a circus of it; tell me later, when . . .

JULIA

War, marriage, money, children . . .

AGNES

You needn't!

JULIA

You! Daddy! Government! Claire—if he'd met her . . . everything!

CLAIRE

Well, I doubt he'd dislike *me; I'm* against everything too.

AGNES *(To* JULIA)

You're tired; we'll talk about it after . . .

JULIA *(Sick disgust)*

I've talked about it! I just talked about it!

AGNES *(Quiet boring in)*

I'm sure there's more.

JULIA

There is no more.

AGNES *(Clenched teeth)*

There is a great deal more, and I'll hear it from you later, when we're alone. You have not come to us in your fourth debacle. . . .

JULIA

HE IS OPPOSED! AND THAT IS ALL! TO EVERYTHING!

AGNES *(After a small silence)*

Perhaps after dinner.

JULIA

NO! NOT PERHAPS AFTER DINNER!

TOBIAS

ALL OF YOU! BE STILL!
(Silence)

CLAIRE *(Flat; to* TOBIAS*)*
Are we having our dividend, or are we not?
(Silence; then, a gentle mocking apology)
"All happy families are alike."
*(*HARRY *and* EDNA *appear in the archway, coats on or over arms)*

HARRY *(A little embarrassed)*
Well.

CLAIRE *(Exaggerated bonhomie)*
Well, look who's here!

TOBIAS *(Embarrassed)*
Harry, just in time for a martini. . . .

HARRY
No, no, we're . . . Julia, there you are!

EDNA *(Affectionate commiseration)*
Oh, Julia.

JULIA *(Bravely, nicely)*
Hello there.

AGNES *(On her feet)*
There's just time for a drink before dinner, if my husband will hurry
some. . . .

HARRY
No, we're . . . going home now.

AGNES
(Relief peeking through the surprise)
Oh? Yes?

EDNA
Yes.
(Pause)

AGNES
Well.

(Pause)
If we were any help at all, we . . .

HARRY

To . . . uh, to get our things.
(Silence)
Our clothes, and things.

EDNA

Yes.

HARRY

We'll be back in . . . well, after dinner, so don't . . .

EDNA

An hour or two. It'll take us a while.
(Silence)

HARRY

We'll let ourselves . . . don't bother.
(They start out, tentatively, see that the others are merely staring at them. Exit. Silence)

JULIA

(Controlled, but near tears)
I want my room back! I want my room!

AGNES

(Composed, chilly, standing in the archway)
I believe that dinner is served. . . .

TOBIAS *(Vacant)*

Yes?

AGNES

If any of you have the stomach for it.

CURTAIN

SCENE TWO

(*Same set, after dinner, the same evening* AGNES *and* TOBIAS *to one side,* AGNES *standing* TOBIAS *not;* JULIA *in another corner, not facing them*)

JULIA

(*A statement, directed to neither of them*)
That was, without question, the *ugliest* dinner I have ever sat through.

AGNES (*Seemingly pleased*)
What did you say?

(*No answer*)
Now, what can you mean? Was the ragout not to your pleasure? Did the floating island sink? Watch what you say, for your father is proud of his wines. . . .

JULIA
No! You! Sitting there! Like a combination . . . pope, and . . . "We will not discuss it"; "Claire, be still"; "No, Tobias, the table is not the proper place"; "Julia!" . . . nanny! Like a nanny!

AGNES
When we are dealing with children . . .

JULIA
I must discover, sometime, who you think you are.

AGNES (*Icy*)
You will learn . . . one day.

JULIA
No, more like a drill sergeant! *You* will do this, *you* will not say that.

AGNES
"To keep in shape." Have you heard the expression? Most people misunderstand it, assume it means alteration, when it does not. Maintenance. When we keep something in shape, we maintain its shape—whether we are proud of that shape, or not, is another matter—we keep *it* from falling apart. We do not attempt the impossible. We maintain. We hold.

JULIA

Yes? So?

AGNES *(Quietly)*

I shall . . . keep this family in shape. I shall maintain it; hold it.

JULIA *(A sneer)*

But you won't attempt the impossible.

AGNES *(A smile)*

I shall keep it in shape. If I am a drill sergeant . . . so be it. Since nobody
. . . *really* wants to talk about your latest . . . marital disorder, really wants to
talk *around* it, use it as an excuse for all sorts of horrid little revenges . . . I
think we can at least keep the table . . . unlittered of *that.*

JULIA
(Sarcastic salute, not rising though)

Yes, sir.

AGNES *(Reasonable)*

And, if I shout, it's merely to be heard . . . above the awful din of your
privacies and sulks . . . all of you. I am not being an ogre, am I?

TOBIAS *(Not anxious to argue)*

No, no; very . . . reasonable.

AGNES

If I am a stickler on certain points

(Just as JULIA's *mouth opens to speak)*

—a martinet, as Julia would have it, would you not, sweet? in fact,
were you not about to?—if I am a stickler on points of manners, tim-
ing, tact—the graces, I almost blush to call them—it is simply that
I am the one member of this . . . reasonably happy family blessed and
burdened with the ability to view a situation objectively while I am
in it.

JULIA *(Not really caring)*

What time is it?

AGNES *(A little harder now)*

The double position of seeing not only facts but their implications . . .

TOBIAS

Nearly ten.

AGNES

(Some irritation toward both of them)

. . . the longer view as well as the shorter. There *is* a balance to be maintained, after all, though the rest of you teeter, unconcerned, or uncaring, *assuming* you're on level ground . . . by divine right, I gather, though that is hardly so. And if I must be the fulcrum. . . .

(Sees neither of them is really listening, says in the same tone)

. . . I think I shall have a divorce.

(Smiles to see that her words have had no effect)

TOBIAS *(It sinks in)*

Have what? A *what?*

AGNES

No fear; merely testing. Everything is taken for granted and no one listens.

TOBIAS *(Wrinkling his nose)*

Have a divorce?

AGNES

No, no; Julia has them for all of us. Not even separation; that is taken care of, and in life: the gradual . . . demise of intensity, the private preoccupations, the substitutions. We become allegorical, my darling Tobias, as we grow older. The individuality we hold so dearly sinks into crotchet; we see ourselves repeated by those we bring into it all, either by mirror or rejection, honor or fault.

(To herself, really)

I'm not a fool; I'm really not.

JULIA

(Leafing a magazine; clear lack of interest but not insulting)

What's Claire up to?

AGNES

(Walking to TOBIAS, *a hand on his shoulder)*

Really not at all.

TOBIAS *(Looking up; fondness)*

No; really not.

AGNES

(Surprisingly unfriendly; to JULIA)

How would I know what she's doing?

JULIA *(She too)*

Well, you are the fulcrum and all around here, the double vision, the great balancing act. . . .

(Lets it slide away)

AGNES

(A little triste; looking away)

I dare say she's in her room.

JULIA *(Little girl)*

At least she has one.

AGNES

(Swinging around to face her; quite hard)

Well, why don't you run upstairs and claim your goddamn room back! Barricade yourself in there! Push a bureau in front of the door! Take Tobias' pistol while you're at it! Arm yourself!

(A burst from an accordion; CLAIRE appears in the archway, wearing it)

CLAIRE

Barricades? Pistols? Really? So soon?

JULIA

(Giggling in spite of herself)

Oh, Claire . . .

AGNES *(Not amused)*

Claire, will you take off that damned thing!

CLAIRE

"They laughed when I sat down to the accordion." Take it off? No, I will not! This is going to be a festive night—from the smell of it, and sister Claire wants to do her part—pay her way, so to speak . . . justify.

AGNES

You're not going to play that dreadful instrument in here, and . . .

(But the rest of what she wants to say is drowned out by a chord from the accordion)

Tobias?

(Calm)

Do something about that.

TOBIAS *(He, too, chuckling)*

Oh, now, Agnes . . .

CLAIRE

So . . .

(Another chord)

. . . shall I wait? Shall I start now? A polka? What?

AGNES *(Icy, but to* TOBIAS*)*

My sister is not *really* lazy. The things she has learned since leaving the nest!: gaucherie, ingratitude, drunkenness, and even . . . this. She has become a musician, too.

CLAIRE *(A twang in her voice)*

Maw used to say: "Claire, girl" . . . she had an uncle named Claire, so she always called me Claire-girl—

AGNES *(No patience with it)*

That is not so.

CLAIRE

"Claire girl," she used to say, "when you go out into the world, get dumped outa the nest, or pushed by your sister . . ."

AGNES *(Steady, but burning)*

Lies.

(Eyes slits)

She kept you, allowed you . . . tolerated! Put up with your filth, your . . . "emancipated womanhood."

(To JULIA, *overly sweet)*

Even in her teens, your Auntie Claire had her own and very special ways, was very . . . advanced.

CLAIRE *(Laughs)*

Had a ball, the same as you, 'cept I wasn't puce with socially proper remorse every time.

(To JULIA*)*

Your mommy got her pudenda scuffed a couple times herself 'fore she met old Toby, you know.

TOBIAS

Your what?

AGNES *(Majesty)*

My pudenda.

CLAIRE *(A little grumpy)*
You can come on all forgetful in your old age, if you want to, but just remember . . .

AGNES *(Quiet anger)*
I am not an old woman.
(Sudden thought; to TOBIAS*)*
Am I?

TOBIAS *(No help; great golly-gosh)*
Well, you're my old lady. . . .
*(*AGNES *almost says something, changes her mind, shakes her head, laughs softly)*

CLAIRE *(A chord)*
Well, what'll it be?

JULIA *(Glum)*
Save it for Harry and Edna.

CLAIRE
Save it for Harry and Edna? Save it for them?
(Chord)

AGNES *(Nice)*
Please.

CLAIRE
All right; I'll unload.
(Removes accordion)

AGNES
I dare say.
(Stops)

TOBIAS
What?

AGNES
No. Nothing.

CLAIRE *(Half-smile)*
We're waiting, aren't we?

TOBIAS
Hm?

CLAIRE

Waiting. The room; the doctor's office; beautiful unconcern; intensive study of the dreadful curtains; absorption in *Field and Stream,* waiting for the Bi-op-*see.*

(Looks from one to the other)

No? Don't know what I mean?

JULIA *(Rather defiant)*

What *about* Harry and Edna?

CLAIRE *(Echo; half-smile)*

We don't want to talk about it.

AGNES

If they come back . . .

CLAIRE

If!?

AGNES *(Closes her eyes briefly)*

If they come back . . . we will . . .

(Shrugs)

CLAIRE

You've only got two choices, Sis. You take 'em in, or you throw 'em out.

AGNES

Ah, how simple it is from the sidelines.

TOBIAS *(Sees through the window)*

We'll do neither, I'd imagine. Take in; throw out.

CLAIRE

Oh?

TOBIAS *(A feeling of nakedness)*

Well, yes, they're just . . . passing through.

CLAIRE

As they have been . . . all these years.

AGNES

Well, we shall know soon enough.

(Not too much pleasure)

They're back.

TOBIAS

(*Rises, goes to the window with her*)

Yes?

JULIA

I think I'll go up . . .

AGNES

You stay right here!

JULIA

I want to go to my . . .

AGNES

It is their room! For the moment.

JULIA (*Not nice*)

Among Doug's opinions, you might like to know, is that when you and your ilk are blown to pieces by a Chinese bomb, the world will be a better place.

CLAIRE

Isn't ilk a lovely word?

AGNES (*Dry*)

You choose well, Julia.

JULIA

(*Retreating into uncertainty*)

That's what he says.

AGNES

Have, always. Did he include *you* as ilk, as well? Will you be with us when "the fatal mushroom" comes. Are we to have the pleasure?

JULIA

(*After a pause; as much a threat as a promise*)

I'll be right here.

TOBIAS

Agnes!

JULIA

Would you like to know something else he says?

AGNES *(Patiently)*

No, Julia.

JULIA

Dad?

TOBIAS *(Some apology in it)*

Not right this minute, Julia. They have gone around to the back.

JULIA *(Defiance)*

Claire? You?

CLAIRE

Well, come on! You *know* I'd like to hear about it—love to—but Toby and Ag've got an invasion on their hands, and . . .

AGNES

We have no such thing.

CLAIRE

. . . and maybe you'd better save it for Harry and Edna, too.

AGNES

It does not concern Edna and Harry.

CLAIRE

Best friends.

AGNES

Tobias?

TOBIAS

(Reluctantly on his feet)

Where . . . what do you want me to do with everything? Every . . . ?

AGNES

(Heading toward the archway)

Well for God's sake! I'll do it.

(They exit)

JULIA

(As CLAIRE moves to the sideboard)

What . . . what do they want? Harry and Edna.

CLAIRE *(Pouring for herself)*

Hmm?

JULIA

You'll make Mother mad. Harry and Edna: what do they want?

CLAIRE

Succor.

JULIA *(Tiny pause)*

Pardon?

CLAIRE *(Brief smile)*

Comfort.

(Sees JULIA *doesn't understand)*

Warmth. A special room with a night light, or the door ajar so you can look down the hall from the bed and see that Mommy's door is open.

JULIA *(No anger; loss)*

But that's my room.

CLAIRE

It's . . . the *room*. Happens you were in it. You're a visitor as much as anyone, now.

(We hear mumbled conversation from the hallway)

JULIA *(Small whine)*

But I *know* that room.

CLAIRE *(Pointed, but kind)*

Are you home for good now?

*(*JULIA *stares at her)*

Are you home forever, back from the world? To the sadness *and* reassurance of your parents? Have you come to take my place?

JULIA *(Quiet despair)*

This is my home!

CLAIRE

This . . . ramble? Yes?

(Surprised delight)

You're laying claim to the cave! Well, I don't know how they'll take to that. We're not a communal nation, dear;

*(*EDNA *appears in the archway, unseen)*

giving, but not sharing, outgoing, but not friendly.

EDNA

Hello.

CLAIRE

(*Friendly, but not turning to look at her*)
Hello!

(*Back to* JULIA)
We submerge our truths and have our sunsets on untroubled waters.
C'mon in, Edna.

EDNA

Yes.

CLAIRE (*Back to* JULIA)
We live with our truths in the grassy bottom, and we examine aalllll the
interpretations of aalllll the implications like we had a life for nothing
else, for God's sake.

(*Turns to* EDNA)
Do *you* think we can walk on the water, Edna? Or do you think we sink?

EDNA (*Dry*)
We sink.

CLAIRE

And we better develop gills. Right?

EDNA

Right. We drove around the back. Harry is helping Agnes and Tobias get
our bags upstairs.

JULIA

(*Slight schoolteacher tone*)
Don't you mean Agnes and Tobias are helping Harry?

EDNA (*Tired*)
If you like.

(*To* CLAIRE)
What were you two up to?

CLAIRE

I think Julia is home for good this time.

JULIA

(*Annoyed and embarrassed*)
For Christ's sake, Claire!

EDNA
(Rather as if JULIA *were not in the room)*
Oh? Is it come to that?

CLAIRE
I always said she would, finally.

JULIA
(Under her breath, to CLAIRE*)*
This is family business!

EDNA *(Looking around the room)*
Yes, but I'm not sure Agnes and Tobias have seen it as clearly. I do wish
Agnes would have that chair recovered. Perhaps now . . .

JULIA *(Exploding)*
Well, why don't you call the upholsterers! Now that you're living here!

CLAIRE *(Quiet amusement)*
All in the family.

EDNA
You're not a child anymore, Julia, you're nicely on your way to forty, and
you've not helped . . . wedlock's image any, with your . . . shenanigans . . .

JULIA *(Full, quivering rage)*
YOU ARE A GUEST IN THIS HOUSE!!

EDNA
(Lets a moment pass, continues quietly)
. . . and if you *have* decided to . . .
(Wistful)
return forever? . . . then it's a matter of some concern for quite a few
peo—

JULIA
You are a *guest!*

CLAIRE *(Quietly)*
As you.

EDNA
. . . for quite a few people . . . whose lives are . . . moved—if not necessarily touched—by your actions. Claire, where does Agnes have her uphol-
stery done? Does she use . . .

JULIA

NO!

EDNA *(Strict, soft and powerful)*
Manners, young lady!

CLAIRE *(Pointed)*
Julia, why don't you ask Edna if she'd like something?

JULIA *(Mouth agape for a moment)*
NO!
(To EDNA*)*
You have no rights here. . . .

EDNA

I'll have a cognac, Julia.
*(*JULIA *stands stock still.* EDNA *continues; precise and pointed)*
My husband and I are your parents' best friends. We are, in addition,
your godparents.

JULIA

DOES THIS GIVE YOU RIGHTS?!

CLAIRE *(Smile)*
Some.

EDNA

Some. Rights and responsibilities. Some.

CLAIRE

(Seeing HARRY *in the archway)*
Hello, there, Harry; c'mon in. Julia's about to fix us all something. What'll
you . . .

HARRY

(Rubbing his hands together; quite at ease)
I'll do it; don't trouble yourself, Julia.

JULIA

*(Rushes to the sideboard, her back to it, spreads her arms, pro-
tecting it, curiously disturbed and frightened by something)*
No! Don't you come near it! Don't you take a step!

HARRY

(Patiently, moving forward a little)
Now, Julia . . .

JULIA

NO!

EDNA *(Sitting relaxing)*

Let her do it, Harry. She wants to.

JULIA

I DON'T WANT TO!!

HARRY *(Firm)*

Then I'll do it, Julia.

JULIA *(Suddenly a little girl; crying)*

Mother!? MOTHER!?

EDNA

(Shaking her head; not unkindly)

Honestly.

JULIA

MOTHER!?

CLAIRE

(The way a nurse speaks to a disturbed patient)

Julia? Will you let me do it? May I get the drinks?

JULIA *(Hissed)*

Stay away from it! All of you!

CLAIRE *(Rising)*

Now, Julia . . .

HARRY

Oh, come on, Julie, now . . .

EDNA

Let her go, Harry.

JULIA

MOTHER? FATHER! HELP ME!!

(AGNES enters)

AGNES *(Pained)*

Julia? You're shouting?

JULIA

Mother!

AGNES *(Quite conscious of the others)*
What *is* it, dear?

JULIA
(Quite beside herself seeing no sympathy)
THEY! THEY WANT!

EDNA
Forget it, Julia.

HARRY
(A tiny, condescending laugh)
Yes, for God's sake, forget it.

JULIA
THEY WANT!

AGNES
(Kindly, but a little patronizing)
Perhaps you *had* better go upstairs.

JULIA *(Still semi-hysterical)*
Yes? Where!? What room!?

AGNES *(Patient)*
Go up to my room, lie down.

JULIA *(An ugly laugh)*
Your room!

EDNA *(Calm)*
You may lie down in *our* room, if you prefer.

JULIA
(A trapped woman, surrounded)
Your room!
(To AGNES)
Your room? MINE!!
(Looks from one to another, sees only waiting faces)
MINE!!

HARRY
(Makes a move toward the sideboard)
God.

JULIA

Don't you go near *that!*

AGNES

Julia . . .

JULIA

I *want!*

CLAIRE *(Sad smile)*

What do you want, Julia?

JULIA

I . . .

HARRY

Jesus.

JULIA

I WANT . . . WHAT IS MINE!!

AGNES

(Seemingly dispassionate; after a pause)
Well, then, my dear, you will have to decide what that is, will you not.

JULIA

(A terrified pause; runs from the room)
Daddy? Daddy?
(A silence; HARRY moves to the sideboard, begins to make himself a drink)

AGNES

(As if very little had happened)
Why, I do believe that's the first time she's called on her father in . . .
since her childhood.

CLAIRE

When she used to skin her knees?

AGNES *(A little laugh)*

Yes, and she would come home bloody. I *assumed* she was clumsy, but it
crossed my mind a time or two . . . that she was religious.

EDNA

Praying on the gravel? A penance?

AGNES

(Chuckles, but it covers something else)

Yes. Teddy had just died, I think, and it was an . . . unreal time . . . for a number of us, for me.

(Brief sorrow clearly shown)

Poor little boy.

EDNA

Yes.

AGNES

It was an unreal time: I thought Tobias was out of love with me—or, rather, was tired of it, when Teddy died, as if that had been the string.

HARRY

Would you like something, Edna?

EDNA

(Her eyes on AGNES; *rather dreamy)*

Um-humh.

AGNES

(Not explaining and to none of them, really)

Ah, the things I doubted then: that I was loved—that *I* loved, for that matter!—that Teddy had ever lived at all—my mind, you see. That Julia would be with us long. I think . . . I think I thought Tobias was unfaithful to me then. Was he, Harry?

EDNA

Oh, Agnes.

HARRY *(Unsubtle)*

Come on, Agnes! Of course not! No!

AGNES *(Faint amusement)*

Was he, Claire? That hot summer, with Julia's knees all bloody and Teddy dead? Did my husband . . . cheat on me?

CLAIRE

(Looks at her steadily, toasts her; then)

Ya got me, Sis.

AGNES *(An amen)*

And that will have to do.

EDNA

Poor *Julia.*

AGNES (*Shrugs*)

Julia is a fool. Will you make me a drink, Harry, since you're being Tobias? A Scotch?

HARRY (*Hands* EDNA *a drink*)

Sure thing. Claire?

CLAIRE

Why not.

AGNES (*An overly sweet smile*)

Claire could tell us so much if she cared to, could you not, Claire. Claire, who watches from the sidelines, has seen so very much, has seen us all so clearly, have you not, Claire. You were not named for nothing.

CLAIRE (*A pleasant warning*)

Lay off, Sis.

AGNES

(*Eyes level on* EDNA *and* HARRY; *precisely and not too nicely*)

What do you *want?*

HARRY

(*After a pause and a look at* EDNA)

I don't know what you mean.

EDNA (*Seemingly puzzled*)

Yes.

AGNES (*Eyes narrow*)

What do you *really . . . want?*

CLAIRE

You gonna tell her, Harry?

HARRY

I, *I* don't know what you mean, Claire. Scotch, was it, Agnes?

AGNES

I *said.*

HARRY (*Less than pleasant*)

Yes, but I don't remember.

EDNA (*Her eyes narrowing too*)

Don't talk to Harry like that.

AGNES

(About to attack, thinks better of it)

I . . . I'm sorry, Edna. I forgot that you're . . . very frightened people.

EDNA

DON'T YOU MAKE FUN OF US!

AGNES

My dear Edna, I am not mak—

EDNA

YES YOU ARE! YOU'RE MAKING FUN OF US.

AGNES

I assure you, Edna . . .

HARRY

(Handing AGNES *a drink; with some disgust)*

Here's your drink.

AGNES

I, I assure you.

CLAIRE *(Putting on her accordion)*

I think it's time for a little music, don't you, kids! I yodel a little, too, nowadays, if anybody . . .

AGNES *(Exasperated)*

We *don't* want music, Claire!

HARRY *(Horrified and amused)*

You, you *what!?* You *yodel!?*

CLAIRE

(As if it were the most natural thing in the world)

Well . . . sure.

EDNA *(Dry)*

Talent will out.

HARRY *(Continuing disbelief)*

You yodel!

CLAIRE *(Emphatic; baby talk)*

'ES!

*(*TOBIAS *has appeared in the archway)*

HARRY

She yodels!

CLAIRE *(Bravura)*

What would ya like, Harry? A chorus of "Take me to the greenhouse, lay me down . . ."?

AGNES

Claire!

TOBIAS

I . . . I wonder if, before the concert, one of you would mind telling me why, uh, my daughter is upstairs, in hysterics?

CLAIRE

Envy, baby; she don't sing, or nothin'.
   (A chord)

TOBIAS

PLEASE!
   (To the others)
Well? Will any of you tell me?

AGNES *(Controlled)*

What, what was she doing, Tobias?

TOBIAS

I told you! She's in hysterics!

AGNES *(Tight smile)*

That is a condition; I inquired about an action.

EDNA *(More sincere than before)*

Poor Julia.

HARRY

I don't understand that girl.

TOBIAS *(Quite miffed)*

An action? Is that what you want? O.K., how about
   (Demonstrates this)
pressed against a corner of the upstairs hall, arms wide, palms back? Eyes darting? Wide?
   (EDNA shakes her head)
How about tearing into Harry and Edna's room . . . ripping the clothes from the closets, hangers and all on the floor? The same for the bureaus?

AGNES *(Steady)*

I see.

TOBIAS

More?

AGNES *(Steady)*

All right.

TOBIAS

Or into your room next? Twisted on your bed, lots of breathing and the great wide eyes? The spread all gathered under her, your big lace pillow in her arms—like a lover—her eyes wide open, no tears now? Though if you come near her the sounds start and you think she'll scream if you touch her?

(Pause)

How's that?

CLAIRE *(Pause)*

Pretty good.

AGNES *(Pause)*

And accurate, I imagine.

TOBIAS *(Daring her)*

You're damned right! Now, why?

AGNES

(To TOBIAS *with a sad smile, ironic)*

Would it seem . . . incomplete to you, my darling, were I to tell you Julia is upset that Har—Edna and Harry are here, that . . .

HARRY *(Arms wide, helplessly)*

I was making myself a drink, for God's sake. . . .

EDNA

I asked her to *make* me something. . . .

TOBIAS

Oh, come on!

EDNA *(Some pleasure)*

She rose . . . like a silent film star, ran to the sideboard, defended it, like a princess in the movies, hiding her lover in the closet from the king.

CLAIRE

That sound incomplete to you, Toby?

TOBIAS *(Stern)*

Somewhat.

AGNES

Julia *has* been through a trying time, Tobias. . . .

HARRY *(A little apologetic)*

I suppose we did upset her some . . . .

EDNA *(Consoling)*

Of course!

TOBIAS

(To AGNES; *a kind of wondrous bewilderment)*
Don't you think you should go tend to her?
(The others all look to AGNES)

AGNES *(Shakes her head; lightly)*

No. She will be down or she will not. She will stop, or she will . . . go on.

TOBIAS *(Spluttering)*

Well, for God's sake, Agnes . . . !

AGNES *(An end to it; hard)*

I haven't the time, Tobias.
(Gentler)
I haven't time for the four-hour talk, the soothing recapitulation. You don't go through it, my love: the history. Nothing is calmed by a pat on the hand, a gentle massage, or slowly, slowly combing the hair, no: the history. Teddy's birth, and how she felt unwanted, tricked; his death, and was she more relieved than lost . . . ? All the schools we sent her to, and did she fail in them through hate . . . or love? And when we come to marriage, dear: each one of them, the fear, the happiness, the sex, the stopping, the infidelities . . .

TOBIAS *(Nodding; speaks softly)*

All right, Agnes.

AGNES *(Shakes her head)*

Oh, my dear Tobias . . . my life is gone through more than hers. I see myself . . . growing old each time, see my own life passing. No, I haven't time for it now. At midnight, maybe . . .
(Sad smile)
when you're all in your beds . . . safely sleeping. Then I will comfort our Julia, and lose myself once more.

CLAIRE

(To break an uncomfortable silence)
I tell ya, there are so many martyrdoms here.

EDNA *(Seeing a hangnail)*
One to a person.

AGNES *(Dry)*
That is the usual,

(A glance at CLAIRE*)*
though I do believe there are some with none, and others who have known Job. The helpless are the cruelest lot of all: they shift their burdens so.

CLAIRE
If you interviewed a camel, he'd admit he loved his load.

EDNA *(Giving up on the hangnail)*
I wish you two would stop having at each other.

HARRY
Hell, yes! Let's have a drink, Tobias?

TOBIAS *(From deep in thought)*
Hm?

HARRY
What can I make yuh, buddy?

CLAIRE *(Rather pleased)*
Why, Edna; you've actually spoken your mind.

TOBIAS *(Confused as to where he is)*
What can *you* make *me?*

EDNA
I do . . . sometimes.

HARRY
Well, sure; I'm here.

EDNA *(Calm)*
When an environment is not all that it might be.

TOBIAS
Oh. Yeah; Scotch.

AGNES (*Strained smile*)

Is that for you to say?

CLAIRE (*A chord; then*)

Here we come!

AGNES

Stop it, Claire, dear.

(*To* EDNA)

I said: Is that for you to say?

EDNA (*To* AGNES; *calm, steady*)

We must be helpful when we can, my dear; that is the . . . responsibility, the double demand of friendship . . . is it not?

AGNES (*Slightly schoolteacherish*)

But, when we are *asked.*

EDNA

(*Shakes her head, smiles gently*)

No. Not only.

(*This heard by all*)

It seemed to me, to us, that since we were living *here* . . .

(*Silence,* AGNES *and* TOBIAS *look from* EDNA *to* HARRY)

CLAIRE

That's my cue!

(*A chord, then begins to yodel, to an ump-pah base.* JULIA *appears in the archway, unseen by the others; her hair is wild, her face is tear-streaked; she carries* TOBIAS' *pistol, but not pointed; awkwardly and facing down*)

JULIA (*Solemnly and tearfully*)

Get them out of here, Daddy, getthemoutofheregetthemoutofhereget-themoutofheregetthemoutofheregetthemoutofhere. . . .

(*They all see* JULIA *and the gun simultaneously;* EDNA *gasps but does not panic;* HARRY *retreats a little;* TOBIAS *moves slowly toward* JULIA)

AGNES

Julia!

JULIA

Get them out of here, Daddy!

TOBIAS

(*Moving toward her, slowly, calmly, speaking in a quiet voice*)
All right, Julia, baby; let's have it now. . . .

JULIA

Get them out of here, Daddy. . . .

TOBIAS (*As before*)

Come on now, Julia.

JULIA

(*Calmly, she hands the gun to* TOBIAS, *nods*)
Get them out of here, Daddy.

AGNES (*Soft intensity*)

You ought to be horsewhipped, young lady.

TOBIAS

(*meant for both* JULIA *and* AGNES)
All right, now . . .

JULIA

Do it, Daddy? Or give it back?

AGNES (*Turns on* JULIA; *withering*)

How dare you come into this room like that! How dare you embarrass
me and your father! How dare you frighten Edna and Harry! How dare
you come into this room like that!

JULIA

(*To* HARRY *and* EDNA; *venom*)
Are you going?

AGNES

Julia!

TOBIAS (*Pleading*)

Julia, please. . . .

JULIA

ARE YOU!?
(*Silence, all eyes on* HARRY *and* EDNA)

EDNA

(*Finally; curiously unconcerned*)
Going? No, we are not going.

HARRY

No.

JULIA *(To all)*

YOU SEE!?

HARRY

Coming down here with a gun like that . . .

EDNA *(Becoming* AGNES*)*

You return to your nest from your latest disaster, dispossessed, and suddenly dispossessing; screaming the house down, clawing at order . . .

JULIA

STOP HER!

EDNA

. . . willful, wicked, wretched girl . . .

JULIA

You are not my . . . YOU HAVE NO RIGHTS!

EDNA

We have rights here. *We* belong.

JULIA

MOTHER!

AGNES *(Tentative)*

Julia . . .

EDNA

We belong here, do we not?

JULIA *(Triumphant distaste)*

FOREVER!!
   (Small silence)
HAVE YOU COME TO STAY FOREVER??
   (Small silence)

EDNA

   (Walks over to her, calmly slaps her)
If need be.
   (To TOBIAS *and* AGNES, *calmly)*
Sorry; a godmother's duty.

(This next calm, almost daring addressed at, rather than to the others)

If we come to the point . . . we are at home one evening, and the . . . terror comes . . . descends . . . *if* all at once we . . . NEED . . . we come where we are wanted, where we know we are expected, not only where we want; we come where the table has been laid for us in such an event . . . where the bed is turned down . . . and warmed . . . and has been ready should we need it. We are not . . . transients . . . like some.

JULIA

NO!

EDNA (To JULIA)

You must . . . what is the word? . . . coexist, my dear.

(To the others)

Must she not?

(Silence; calm)

Must she not. This is what you have meant by friendship . . . is it not?

AGNES (Pause; finally, calmly)

You have come to live with us, then.

EDNA (After a pause; calm)

Why, yes; we have.

AGNES (Dead calm; a sigh)

Well, then.

(Pause)

Perhaps it is time for bed, Julia? Come upstairs with me.

JULIA (A confused child)

M-mother?

AGNES

Ah-ah; let me comb your hair, and rub your back.

(Arm over JULIA*'s shoulder, leads her out. Exiting)*

And we shall soothe . . . and solve . . . and fall to sleep. Tobias?

(Exits with JULIA*. Silence)*

EDNA

Well, I think it's time for bed.

TOBIAS *(Vague, preoccupied)*
Well, yes; yes, of course.

EDNA
(She and HARRY *have risen; a small smile)*
We know the way.
(Pauses as she and HARRY *near the archway)*
Friendship *is* something like a marriage, is it not, Tobias? For better and
for worse?

TOBIAS *(Ibid.)*
Sure.

EDNA *(Something of a demand here)*
We *haven't* come to the wrong place, *have* we?

HARRY *(Pause; shy)*
Have we, Toby?

TOBIAS *(Pause; gentle, sad)*
No.
(Sad smile)
No; of course you haven't.

EDNA
Good night, dear Tobias. Good night, Claire.

CLAIRE *(A half smile)*
Good night, you two.

HARRY
(A gentle pat at TOBIAS *as he passes)*
Good night, old man.

TOBIAS *(Watches as the two exit)*
Good . . . good night, you two.
*(*CLAIRE *and* TOBIAS *alone;* TOBIAS *still holds the pistol)*

CLAIRE *(After an interval)*
Full house, Tobias, every bed and every cupboard.

TOBIAS *(Not moving)*
Good night, Claire.

CLAIRE *(Rising leaving her accordion)*
Are you going to stay up, Tobias? Sort of a nightwatch, guarding? *I've
done it.* The breathing, as you stand in the quiet halls, slow and heavy?
And the special . . . warmth, and . . . permeation . . . of a house . . . asleep?
When the house is sleeping? When the people *are* asleep?

TOBIAS
Good night, Claire.

CLAIRE *(Near the archway)*
And the difference? The different breathing and the cold, when every
bed is awake . . . all night . . . very still, eyes open, staring into the dark?
Do you know that one?

TOBIAS
Good night, Claire.

CLAIRE *(A little sad)*
Good night, Tobias.
      (Exit as the curtain falls)

ACT THREE

(*Seven-thirty the next morning; same set.* TOBIAS *alone, in a chair, wearing pajamas and a robe, slippers. Awake.* AGNES *enters, wearing a dressing gown which could pass for a hostess gown. Her movements are not assertive, and her tone is gentle*)

AGNES (*Seeing him*)

Ah; there you are.

TOBIAS

(*Not looking at her, but at his watch; there is very little emotion in his voice*)

Seven-thirty A.M., and all's well . . . I guess.

AGNES

So odd.

TOBIAS

Hm?

AGNES

There was a stranger in my room last night.

TOBIAS

Who?

AGNES

You.

TOBIAS

Ah.

AGNES

It was nice to have you there.

TOBIAS (*Slight smile*)

Hm.

AGNES

Le temps perdu. I've never understood that; *perdu* means lost, not merely . . . past, but it was nice to have you there, though I remember, when it was a constancy, how easily I would fall asleep, pace my breathing to your breathing, and if we were touching! ah, what a splendid cocoon that was. But last night—what a shame, what sadness—you were a stranger, and I stayed awake.

TOBIAS

I'm sorry.

AGNES

Were you asleep at all?

TOBIAS

No.

AGNES

I would go half, then wake—your unfamiliar presence, sir. I *could* get used to it again.

TOBIAS

Yes?

AGNES

I think.

TOBIAS

You didn't have your talk with Julia—your all-night lulling.

AGNES

No; she wouldn't let me stay. "Look to your own house," is what she said. You stay down long?

TOBIAS

When?

AGNES

After . . . before you came to bed.

TOBIAS

Some.
    (Laughs softly, ruefully)
I almost went into *my* room . . . by habit . . . by mistake, rather, but then I realized that your room is my room because my room is Julia's because Julia's room is . . .

AGNES

. . . yes.
    (Goes to him, strokes his temple)
And I was awake when you left my room again.

TOBIAS *(Gentle reproach)*

You could have said.

AGNES *(Curious at the truth)*

I felt shy.

TOBIAS *(Pleased surprise)*

Hm!

AGNES

Did you go to Claire?

TOBIAS

I never go to Claire.

AGNES

Did you go to Claire to talk?

TOBIAS

I never go to Claire.

AGNES

We must always envy someone we should not, be jealous of those who have so much less. You and Claire make so much sense together, talk so well.

TOBIAS

I never go to Claire at night, or talk with her alone—save publicly.

AGNES *(Small smile)*

In public rooms . . . like this.

TOBIAS

Yes.

AGNES

Have *never.*

TOBIAS

Please?

AGNES

Do we dislike happiness? We manufacture such a portion of our own despair . . . such busy folk.

TOBIAS

We are a highly moral land: we assume we have done great wrong. We find the things.

AGNES

I shall start missing you again—when you move from my room . . . if you do. I had stopped, I believe.

TOBIAS (*Grudging little chuckle*)
Oh, you're an honest woman.

AGNES
Well, we need *one* . . . in every house.

TOBIAS
It's very strange . . . to be downstairs, in a room where everyone has been, and is gone . . . very late, after the heat has gone—the furnace *and* the bodies: the hour or two before the sun comes up, the furnace starts again. And tonight especially: the cigarettes still in the ashtrays—odd, metallic smell. The odors of a room don't mix, late, when there's no one there, and I think the silence helps it . . . and the lack of bodies. Each . . . thing stands out in its place.

AGNES
What did you decide?

TOBIAS
And when you *do* come down . . . if you do, at three, or four, and you've left a light or two—in case someone should come in late, I suppose, but who is there left? The inn is full—it's rather . . . Godlike, if I may presume: to look at it all, reconstruct, with such . . . de*tach*ment, see your*self* you, Julia . . . Look at it all . . . play it out again, *watch*.

AGNES
Judge?

TOBIAS
No; that's being in it. Watch. And if you have a drink or two . . .

AGNES (*Mild surprise*)
Did you?

TOBIAS (*Nods*)
And if you have a drink or two, very late, in the quiet, tired, the mind . . . lets loose.

AGNES
Yes?

TOBIAS
And you watch it as it reasons, all with a kind of . . . grateful delight, at the same time sadly, 'cause you know that when the daylight comes the pressures will be on, and all the insight won't be worth a damn.

AGNES
What did you decide?

TOBIAS

You can sit and watch. You can have . . . so clear a picture, see everybody moving through his own jungle . . . an insight into all the reasons, all the needs.

AGNES

Good. And what did you decide?

TOBIAS *(No complaint)*

Why is the room so dirty? Can't we have better servants, some help who . . . help?

AGNES

They keep far better hours than we, that's all. They are a comment on our habits, a reminder that we are out of step—that is why we pay them . . . so very, very much. Neither a servant nor a master be. Remember?

TOBIAS

I remember when . . .

AGNES *(Picking it right up)*

. . . you were very young and lived at home, and the servants were awake whenever you were: six A.M. for your breakfast when you wanted it, or five in the morning when you came home drunk and seventeen, washing the vomit from the car, and you, telling no one; stealing just enough each month, by arrangement with the stores, to keep them in a decent wage; generations of them: the laundress, blind and always dying, and the cook, who did a better dinner drunk than sober. Those servants? Those days? When you were young, and lived at home?

TOBIAS *(Memory)*

Hmmm.

AGNES *(Sweet; sad)*

Well, my darling, you are not young now, and you do not live at home.

TOBIAS *(Sad question)*

Where do I live?

AGNES *(An answer of sorts)*

The dark sadness. Yes?

TOBIAS *(Quiet, rhetorical)*

What are we going to do?

AGNES

What did you decide?

TOBIAS *(Pause; they smile)*

Nothing.

AGNES

Well, you must. Your house is not in order, sir. It's full to bursting.

TOBIAS

Yes. You've got to help me here.

AGNES

No. I don't *think* so.

TOBIAS *(Some surprise)*

No?

AGNES

No. I thought a little last night, too: while you were seeing everything so clearly here. I lay in the dark, and I . . . revisited—our life, the years and years. There are many things a woman does: she bears the children—if there *is* that blessing. Blessing? Yes, I suppose, even with the sadness. She runs the house, for what that's worth: makes sure there's food, and not just anything, and decent linen; looks well; assumes whatever duties are demanded—if she is in love, or loves; and plans.

TOBIAS

(Mumbled; a little embarrassed)

I know, I know. . . .

AGNES

And plans. Right to the end of it; expects to be alone one day, abandoned by a heart attack or the cancer, *prepares* for that. And prepares earlier, for the children to become *adult* strangers instead of growing ones, for that loss, and for the body chemistry, the end of what the Bible tells us is our usefulness. The reins we hold! It's a team of twenty horses, and we sit there, and we watch the road and check the leather . . . if our . . . man is so disposed. But there are things we do not do.

TOBIAS *(Slightly edgy challenge)*

Yes?

AGNES

Yes.

(Harder)
We don't decide the route.

TOBIAS

You're copping out . . . as they say.

AGNES

No, indeed.

TOBIAS *(Quiet anger)*

Yes, you are!

AGNES *(Quiet warning)*

Don't you yell at me.

TOBIAS

You're copping *out!*

AGNES

(Quiet, calm, and almost smug)
We follow. We let our . . . men decide the moral issues.

TOBIAS *(Quite angry)*

Never! You've never done that in your life!

AGNES

Always, my darling. Whatever you decide . . . I'll make it work; I'll run it
for you so you'll never know there's been a change in anything.

TOBIAS

(Almost laughing; shaking his head)
No. No.

AGNES *(To end the discussion)*

So, let me know.

TOBIAS *(Still almost laughing)*

I *know* I'm tired. I know I've hardly slept at all: I know I've sat down
here, and thought . . .

AGNES

And made your decisions.

TOBIAS

But I have not *judged.* I told you that.

AGNES *(Almost a stranger)*
Well, when you have . . . you let me know.

TOBIAS *(Frustration and anger)*
NO!

AGNES *(Cool)*
You'll wake the house.

TOBIAS *(Angry)*
I'll wake the house!

AGNES
This is not the time for you to lose control.

TOBIAS
I'LL LOSE CONTROL! I have *sat* here . . . in the cold, in the empty
cold, I have sat here alone, and . . .
  (Anger has shifted to puzzlement, complaint)
I've looked at *every*thing, *all* of it. I thought of you, and Julia, and Claire. . . .

AGNES *(Still cool)*
And Edna? And Harry?

TOBIAS *(Tiny pause; then anger)*
Well, of course! What do you think!

AGNES *(Tiny smile)*
I don't know. I'm listening.
  *(*JULIA *appears in the archway; wears a dressing gown; subdued,
  sleepy)*

JULIA
Good morning. I don't suppose there's . . . shall I make some coffee?

AGNES *(Chin high)*
Why don't you do that, darling.

TOBIAS *(A little embarrassed)*
Good morning, Julie.

JULIA *(Hating it)*
I'm sorry about last night, Daddy.

TOBIAS
Oh, well, now . . .

JULIA *(Bite to it)*
I mean I'm sorry for having embarrassed you.
(Starts toward the hallway)

AGNES
Coffee.

JULIA
(Pausing at the archway; to TOBIAS*)*
Aren't you sorry for embarrassing me, too?
(Waits a moment, smiles, exits. Pause)

AGNES
Well, isn't that nice that Julia's making coffee? No? If the help aren't up, isn't it nice to have a daughter who can put a pot to boil?

TOBIAS
(Under his breath, disgusted)
"Aren't you sorry for embarrassing me, too."

AGNES
You have a problem there with Julia.

TOBIAS
I? I have a problem!

AGNES
Yes.
(Gentle irony)
But at least you have your women with you—crowded 'round, firm arm, support. *That* must be a comfort to you. *Most* explorers go alone, don't have their families with them—pitching tents, tending the fire, shooing off the . . . the antelopes or the bears or whatever.

TOBIAS *(Wanting to talk about it)*
"Aren't you sorry for embarrassing me, too."

AGNES
Are you quoting?

TOBIAS
Yes.

AGNES
Next we'll have my sister with us—another porter for the dreadful trip.

(Irony)
Claire has never missed a chance to participate in watching. She'll be
here. We'll have us all.

TOBIAS
And you'll all sit down and watch me carefully; smoke your pipes and stir
the cauldron; watch.

AGNES *(Dreamy; pleased)*
Yes.

TOBIAS
You, who make all the decisions, really rule the game . . .

AGNES *(So patient)*
That is an *illusion* you have.

TOBIAS
You'll all sit here—too early for . . . *anything* on this . . . stupid Sunday—
all of you and . . . and *dare* me?—when it's just as much your choice as
mine?

AGNES
Each time that Julia comes, each clockwork time . . . do you send her
back? Do you tell her, "Julia, go home to your husband, try it again"? Do
you? No, you let it . . . slip. It's your decision, sir.

TOBIAS
It is not! I . . .

AGNES
. . . and I must live with it, resign myself one marriage more, and wait,
and hope that Julia's motherhood will come . . . one day, one marriage.
(Tiny laugh)
I am almost too old to be a grandmother as I'd hoped . . . too young to
be one. Oh, I had wanted that: the *youngest* older woman in the block.
Julia is almost too old to have a child properly, *will* be if she ever does
. . . if she marries again. *You* could have pushed her back . . . if you'd
wanted to.

TOBIAS *(Bewildered incredulity)*
It's very early yet: that must be it. I've never heard such . . .

AGNES
Or Teddy! No? No stammering here? You'll let this pass?

TOBIAS *(Quiet embarrassment)*

Please.

AGNES *(Remorseless)*

When Teddy died?

(Pause)

We *could* have had another son; we could have tried. But no . . . those months—or was it a year—?

TOBIAS

No more of this!

AGNES

. . . I think it was a year, when you spilled yourself on my belly, sir? "Please? Please, Tobias?" No, you wouldn't even say it out: I don't want another child, another loss. "Please? Please, Tobias?" And guiding you, *trying* to hold you in?

TOBIAS *(Tortured)*

Oh, Agnes! Please!

AGNES

"Don't leave me then, like that. Not again, Tobias. Please? *I* can take care of it: we *won't* have another child, but please don't . . . leave me like that." Such . . . silent . . . sad, disgusted . . . love.

TOBIAS *(Mumbled, inaudible)*

I didn't want you to have to.

AGNES

Sir?

TOBIAS *(Numb)*

I didn't want you to have to . . . you know.

AGNES *(Laughs in spite of herself)*

Oh, that was thoughtful of you! Like a pair of adolescents in a rented room, or in the family car. Doubtless you hated it as much as I.

TOBIAS *(Softly)*

Yes.

AGNES

But wouldn't let me help you.

TOBIAS *(Ibid.)*

No.

AGNES *(Irony)*
Which is why you took to your own sweet room instead.

TOBIAS *(Ibid.)*
Yes.

AGNES
The theory being pat: that a half a loaf is worse than none. That you are racked with guilt—stupidly!—and *I* must *suffer* for it.

TOBIAS *(Ibid.)*
Yes?

AGNES *(Quietly; sadly)*
Well, it was your decision, was it not?

TOBIAS *(Ibid.)*
Yes.

AGNES
And I have made the best of it. Have lived with it. Have I not?

TOBIAS *(Pause; a plea)*
What are we going to do? About everything?

AGNES *(Quietly; sadly; cruelly)*
Whatever you like. Naturally.
(Silence. CLAIRE *enters, she, too, in a dressing gown)*

CLAIRE
(Judges the situation for a moment)
Morning, kids.

AGNES
(To TOBIAS, *in reference to* CLAIRE)
All I can do, my dear, is run it for you . . . and forecast.

TOBIAS *(Glum)*
Good morning, Claire.

AGNES
Julia is in the kitchen making coffee, Claire.

CLAIRE
Which means, I guess, I go watch Julia grind the beans and drip the water, hunh?

(Exiting)

I tell ya, she's a real pioneer, that girl: coffee pot in one hand, pistol in t'other.

(Exits)

AGNES *(Small smile)*

Claire is a comfort in the early hours . . . I have been told.

TOBIAS *(A dare)*

Yes?

AGNES

(Pretending not to notice his tone)

That is what I have been *told*.

TOBIAS *(Blurts it out)*

Shall I ask them to leave?

AGNES *(Tiny pause)*

Who?

TOBIAS *(Defiant)*

Harry and Edna?

AGNES *(Tiny laugh)*

Oh. For a moment I thought you meant Julia and Claire.

TOBIAS *(Glum)*

No. Harry and Edna. Shall I throw them out?

AGNES *(Restatement of a fact)*

Harry is your very best friend in the whole . . .

TOBIAS *(Impatient)*

Yes, and Edna is yours. Well?

AGNES

You'll have to live with it either way: do or don't.

TOBIAS *(Anger rising)*

Yes? Well, then, why *don't* I throw Julia and Claire out instead? Or better yet, why don't I throw the whole bunch out!?

AGNES

Or get rid of me! That would be easier: rid yourself of the harridan. Then you can run your mission and take out sainthood papers.

TOBIAS *(Clenched teeth)*

I think you're stating an opinion, a preference.

AGNES

But if you *do* get rid of me . . . you'll no longer have your life the way you want it.

TOBIAS *(Puzzled)*

But that's not my . . . that's not all the choice I've got, is it?

AGNES

I don't care very much what choice you've got, my darling, but I *am* concerned with what choice you *make.*

(JULIA *and* CLAIRE *enter;* JULIA *carries a tray with coffee pot, cups, sugar, cream;* CLAIRE *carries a tray with four glasses of orange juice)*

Ah, here are the helpmeets, what would we do without them.

JULIA *(Brisk, efficient)*

The coffee is instant, I'm afraid; I couldn't find a bean: Those folk must lock them up before they go to bed.

(Finds no place to put her tray down)

Come on, Pop; let's clear away a little of the debris, hunh?

TOBIAS

P-Pop?

AGNES *(Begins clearing)*

It's true: we cannot drink our coffee amidst a sea of last night's glasses. Tobias, do be a help.

(TOBIAS *rises, takes glasses to the sideboard, as* AGNES *moves some to another table)*

CLAIRE *(Cheerful)*

And I didn't have to do a thing; thank God for pre-squeezed orange juice.

JULIA *(Setting the tray down)*

There; now that's much better, isn't it?

TOBIAS *(In a fog)*

Whatever you say, Julie.

(JULIA *pours, knows what people put in)*

CLAIRE

Now, I'll play waiter. Sis?

AGNES

Thank you, Claire.

CLAIRE

Little Julie?

JULIA

Just put it down beside me, Claire. I'm pouring, you can see.

CLAIRE

(Looks at her a moment, does not, offers a glass to TOBIAS*)*
Pop?

TOBIAS *(Bewildered, apprehensive)*

Thank you, Claire.

CLAIRE

(Puts JULIA*'s glass on the mantel)*
Yours is here, daughter, when you've done with playing early-morning hostess.

JULIA

(Intently pouring; does not rise to the bait)
Thank you, Claire.

CLAIRE

Now; one for little Claire.

JULIA *(Still pouring; no expression)*
Why don't you have some vodka in it, Claire? To start the Sunday off?

AGNES *(Pleased chuckle)*

Julia!

TOBIAS *(Reproving)*

Please, Julie!

JULIA *(Looks up at him; cold)*
Did I say something wrong, Father?

CLAIRE

Vodka? Sunday? Ten to eight? Why not!

TOBIAS

(Quietly, as she moves to the sideboard)
You don't *have* to, Claire.

JULIA *(Dropping sugar in a cup)*

Let her do what she wants.

CLAIRE *(Pouring vodka into her glass)*

Yes I *do*, Tobias; the rules of the guestbook—be polite. We have our friends and guests for patterns, don't we?—known quantities. The drunks stay drunk; the Catholics go to Mass, the bounders bound. We can't have changes—throws the balance off.

JULIA *(Ibid.)*

Besides; you like to drink.

CLAIRE

Besides, I like to drink. Just think, Tobias, what would happen if the patterns changed: you wouldn't know where you stood, and the world would be full of strangers; that would never do.

JULIA *(Not very friendly)*

Bring me my orange juice, will you please.

CLAIRE *(Getting it for her)*

Oooh, Julia's back for a spell, I think—settling in.

JULIA *(Handing TOBIAS his coffee)*

Father?

TOBIAS *(Embarrassed)*

Thank you, Julia.

JULIA

Mother?

AGNES *(Comfortable)*

Thank you, darling.

JULIA

Yours is here, Claire; on the tray.

CLAIRE

(Considers a moment, looks at JULIA's orange juice, still in one of her hands, calmly pours it on the rug)

Your juice is here, Julia, when you want it.

AGNES *(Furious)*

CLAIRE!

TOBIAS *(Mild reproach)*

For God's sake, Claire.

JULIA

(*Looks at the mess on the rug; shrugs*)

Well, why not. Nothing changes.

CLAIRE

Besides, our friends upstairs don't like the room; they'll want some alterations.

(CLAIRE *sits down*)

TOBIAS

(*Lurches to his feet; stands, legs apart*)

Now! All of you! Sit down! Shut up. I want to talk to you.

JULIA

Did I give you sugar, Mother?

TOBIAS

BE QUIET, JULIA!

AGNES

Shhh, my darling, yes, you did.

TOBIAS

I want to talk to you.

(*Silence*)

CLAIRE

(*Slightly mocking encouragement*)

Well, go *on*, Tobias.

TOBIAS (*A plea*)

You, too, Claire? Please.

(*Silence. The women stir their coffee or look at him, or at the floor. They seem like children about to be lectured, unwilling, and dangerous, but, for the moment, behaved*)

Now.

(*Pause*)

Now, something happened here last night, and I don't mean Julia's hysterics with the gun—be quiet, Julia!— though I *do* mean that, in part. I mean . . .

(*Deep sigh*)

. . . Harry and Edna . . . coming here . . .

(JULIA *snorts*)

Yes? Did you want to say something, Julia? No? I came down here and I sat, all night—hours—and I did something rather rare for this family: I *thought* about something. . . .

AGNES *(Mild)*

I'm sorry, Tobias, but that's not fair.

TOBIAS *(Riding over)*

I *thought.* I sat down here and I thought about all of us . . . and everything. Now, Harry and Edna have come to us and . . . asked for help.

JULIA

That is not *true.*

TOBIAS

Be quiet!

JULIA

That is not true! They have not *asked* for anything!

AGNES

. . . please, Julia . . .

JULIA

They have *told!* They have come in here and *ordered!*

CLAIRE *(Toasts)*

Just like the family.

TOBIAS

Asked! If you're begging and you've got your pride . . .

JULIA

If you're begging, then you may not have your pride!

AGNES *(Quiet contradiction)*

I don't think that's true, Julia.

CLAIRE

Julia wouldn't know. Ask me.

JULIA *(Adamant)*

Those people have no right!

TOBIAS

No right? All these years? We've known them since . . . for God's sake, Julia, those people are our *friends!*

JULIA *(Hard)*

THEN TAKE THEM IN!
(Silence)
Take these . . . intruders in.

CLAIRE *(To* JULIA: *hard)*
Look, baby; didn't you get the message on rights last night? Didn't you learn about intrusion, what the score is, who belongs?

JULIA *(To* TOBIAS)
You bring these people in here, Father, and I'm leaving!

TOBIAS *(Almost daring her)*
Yes?

JULIA
I don't mean coming and going, Father; I mean as *family!*

TOBIAS *(Frustration and rage)*
HARRY AND EDNA ARE OUR FRIENDS!!

JULIA *(Equal)*
THEY ARE INTRUDERS!!
(Silence)

CLAIRE *(To* TOBIAS, *laughing)*
Crisis sure brings out the best in us, don't it, Tobe? The family circle? Julia standing there . . . *asserting;* perpetual brat, and maybe ready to pull a Claire. *And* poor Claire! Not much help there either, is there? And lookit Agnes, talky Agnes, ruler of the roost, and maître d', *and* licensed wife— silent. All cozy, coffee, thinking of the menu for the week, *planning.* Poor Tobe.

AGNES *(Calm, assured)*
Thank you, Claire; I was merely waiting—until I'd heard, and thought a little, listened to the rest of you. I thought someone should sit back. Especially me: ruler of the roost, licensed wife, midnight . . . nurse. And I've been thinking about Harry and Edna; about disease.

TOBIAS *(After a pause)*
About what?

CLAIRE *(After a swig)*
About disease.

JULIA

Oh, for God's sake . . .

AGNES

About disease—or, if you like, the terror.

CLAIRE *(Chuckles softly)*

Unh, hunh.

JULIA *(Furious)*

TERROR!?

AGNES *(Unperturbed)*

Yes: the terror. Or the plague—they're both the same. Edna and Harry have come to us—dear friends, our very best, though there's a judgment to be made about that, I think—have come to us and brought the plague. Now, poor Tobias has sat up all night and wrestled with the moral problem.

TOBIAS *(Frustration; anger)*

I've not been . . . *wrestling* with some . . . abstract problem! These are *people!* Harry and Edna! These are our friends, God damn it!

AGNES

Yes, but they've brought the plague with them, and that's another matter. Let me tell you something about disease . . . mortal illness; you either are immune to it . . . or you fight it. If you are immune, you wade right in, you treat the patient until he either lives, or dies of it. But if you are *not* immune, you risk infection. Ten centuries ago—and even less—the treatment was quite simple . . . burn them. Burn their bodies, burn their houses, burn their clothes—and move to another town, if you were enlightened. But now, with modern medicine, we merely isolate; we quarantine, we ostracize—if we are not immune ourselves, or unless we are saints. So, your night-long vigil, darling, your reasoning in the cold, pure hours, has been over the patient, and not the illness. It is not Edna and Harry who have come to us—our friends—it is a disease.

TOBIAS

(Quiet anguish, mixed with impatience)

Oh, for God's sake, Agnes! It is our friends! What am I supposed to do? Say: "Look, you can't stay here, you two, you've got trouble. You're friends, and all, but you come in here *clean*." Well, I can't do that. No. Agnes, for God's sake, if . . . if that's all Harry and Edna mean to us, then . . . then what about *us?* When we talk to each other . . . what have we meant? Anything? When we touch, when we promise, and say . . . yes, or please. . . with our*selves?* . . . have we meant, yes, but only if . . . if there's any condition, Agnes! Then it's . . . all been empty.

AGNES *(Noncommittal)*

Perhaps. But blood binds us. Blood holds us together when we've no more . . . deep affection for ourselves than others. I am *not* asking you to choose between your family and . . . our friends . . . .

TOBIAS

Yes you are!

AGNES *(Eyes closed)*

I am merely saying that there is *disease* here! And I ask you: who in this family is immune?

CLAIRE *(Weary statement of fact)*

I am. I've had it. I'm still alive, I think.

AGNES

Claire is the strongest of us all: the walking wounded often are, the least susceptible; but think about the rest of us. Are we immune to it? The plague, my darling, the terror sitting in the room upstairs? Well, if we are, then . . . on with it! And, if we're not . . .

(Shrugs)

well, why not be infected, why not die of it? We're bound to die of something . . . soon, or in a while. Or shall we burn them out, rid ourselves of it all . . . and wait for the next invasion. You decide, my darling.

(Silence. TOBIAS rises, walks to the window; the others sit. HARRY and EDNA appear in the archway, dressed for the day, but not with coats)

EDNA *(No emotion)*

Good morning.

AGNES *(Brief pause)*

Ah, you're up.

CLAIRE

Good morning, Edna, Harry.

(JULIA does not look at them; TOBIAS does, but says nothing)

EDNA

(A deep breath, rather a recitation)

Harry wants to talk to Tobias. I think that they should be alone. Perhaps . . .

AGNES

Of course.

(The three seated women rise, as at a signal, begin to gather the coffee things)

Why don't we all go in the kitchen, make a proper breakfast.

HARRY

Well, now, no; you don't have to . . .

AGNES

Yes, yes, we want to leave you to your talk. Tobias?

TOBIAS *(Quiet)*

Uh . . . yes.

AGNES *(To* TOBIAS; *comfortingly)*

We'll be nearby.

(The women start out)

Did you sleep well, Edna? Did you sleep at all? I've never had that bed, but I know that when . . .

(The women have exited)

HARRY

(Watching them go; laughs ruefully)

Boy, look at 'em go. They got outa *here* quick enough. You'd think there was a . . .

(Trails off sees TOBIAS *is ill at ease; says, gently)*

Morning, Tobias.

TOBIAS *(Grateful)*

Morning, Harry.

(Both men stay standing)

HARRY *(Rubs his hands together)*

You, ah . . . you know what I'd like to do? Something I've never done in my life, except once, when I was about twenty-four?

TOBIAS *(Not trying to guess)*

No? What?

HARRY

Have a drink before breakfast? Is, is that all right?

TOBIAS

(Smiles wanly, moves slowly toward the sideboard)

Sure.

HARRY *(Shy)*

Will you join me?

TOBIAS *(Very young)*

I guess so, yes. There isn't any ice.

HARRY

Well, just some whiskey, then; neat.

TOBIAS

Brandy?

HARRY

No, oh, God, no.

TOBIAS

Whiskey, then.

HARRY

Yes. Thank you.

TOBIAS *(Somewhat glum)*

Well, here's to youth again.

HARRY

Yes.

(Drinks)

Doesn't taste too bad in the morning, does it?

TOBIAS

No, but I had some . . . before.

HARRY

When?

TOBIAS

Earlier . . . oh, three, four, while you all were . . . asleep, or whatever you were doing.

HARRY *(Seemingly casual)*

Oh, you were . . . awake, hunh?

TOBIAS

Yes.

HARRY

I slept a *little*.
   (*Glum laugh*)
God.

TOBIAS

What?

HARRY

You know what I did last night?

TOBIAS

No?

HARRY

I got out of bed and I . . . crawled in with Edna?

TOBIAS

Yes?

HARRY

She held me. She let me stay awhile, then I could see she wanted to, and
I didn't . . . so I went back. But it was funny.

TOBIAS *(Nods)*

Yeah.

HARRY

Do you . . . do you, uh, like Edna . . . Tobias?

TOBIAS *(Embarrassed)*

Well, sure I *like* her, Harry.

HARRY *(Pause)*

Now, Tobias, about last night, and yesterday, and our coming here, now . . .

HARRY	TOBIAS
I was talking about it to Edna, last night, and I said, "Look, Edna, what do we think we're doing."	I sat up all night and I thought about it, Harry, and I talked to Agnes this morning, before you all came down.

HARRY

I'm sorry.

TOBIAS

I said, I sat up all night and I thought about it, Harry, and I talked to
Agnes, too, before you all came down, and . . . By God, it isn't easy, Harry
. . . but we can make it. . . if you want us to . . . . *I* can, I mean, I *think*
I can.

HARRY

No . . . we're . . . we're going, Tobias.

TOBIAS

I don't know what help . . . I don't know *how* . . .

HARRY

I said: we're *going*.

TOBIAS

Yes, but . . . you're going?

HARRY *(Nice, shy smile)*

Sure.

TOBIAS

But, but you can *try* it here . . . or we can, God, I don't know, Harry. You can't go back there; you've got to . . .

HARRY

Got to what? Sell the house? Buy another? Move to the club?

TOBIAS

You came *here!*

HARRY *(Sad)*

Do you *want* us here, Tobias?

TOBIAS

You *came* here.

HARRY

Do you *want* us here?

TOBIAS

You *came! Here!*

HARRY *(Too clearly enunciated)*

Do you want us here?

(Subdued, almost apologetic)

Edna and I . . . there's. . . so much . . . over the dam, so many . . . disappointments, evasions, I guess, lies maybe . . . so much we remember we wanted, once . . . so little that we've . . . settled for . . . we talk, sometimes, but mostly . . . no. We don't . . . "like." Oh, sure, we *like* . . . but I've always been a little shy— gruff, you know, and . . . shy. And Edna isn't . . . happy—I suppose that's it. We . . . we like you and . . . and Agnes, and . . . well Claire, and Julia, too, I guess I mean . . . *I* like you, and you like me, I think, and . . . you're our best friends, but . . . I told Edna upstairs, I said: Edna, what if they'd come to us? And she didn't say anything. And I said: Edna, if they'd come to us like this, and even though we don't have . . . Julia, and all of that, I . . . Edna, I wouldn't take them in.

(Brief silence)

I wouldn't take them in, Edna; they don't . . . they don't have any right. And she said: yes, I know; they wouldn't have the right.

(Brief silence)

Toby, I wouldn't let *you* stay.

(Shy, embarrassed)

You . . . you don't *want* us, do you, Toby? You don't want us here.

TOBIAS

(This next is an aria. It must have in its performance all the horror and exuberance of a man who has kept his emotions under control too long. TOBIAS *will be carried to the edge of hysteria, and he will find himself laughing sometimes, while he cries from sheer release. All in all, it is genuine and bravura at the same time, one prolonging the other. I shall try to notate it somewhat)*

(Softly, and as if the word were unfamiliar)

Want?

(Same)

What? Do I what?

(Abrupt laugh; joyous)

DO I WANT?

(More laughter; also a sob)

DO I WANT YOU HERE!

(Hardly able to speak from the laughter)

You come in here, you come in here with your . . . wife, and with your . . . terror! And you ask me if I want you here!

(Great breathing sounds)

YES! OF COURSE! I WANT YOU HERE! THIS IS MY HOUSE! I WANT YOU IN IT! I WANT YOUR PLAGUE! YOU'VE GOT SOME TERROR WITH YOU? BRING IT IN!

(Pause, then, even louder)

BRING IT IN!! YOU'VE GOT THE
ENTREE, BUDDY, YOU DON'T NEED
A KEY! YOU'VE GOT THE ENTREE,
BUDDY! FORTY YEARS!

(Soft, now; soft and fast, almost a monotone)

You don't need to ask me, Harry, you don't
need to ask a thing; you're our friends,
our very best friends in the world, and
you don't have to ask.

(A shout)

WANT? ASK?

(Soft, as before)

You come for dinner don't you come for
cocktails see us at the club on Saturdays
and talk and lie and laugh with us and pat
old Agnes on the hand and say you don't
know what old Toby'd do without her and
we've known you all these years and we
love each other don't we?

(Shout)

DON'T WE?! DON'T WE LOVE EACH
OTHER?

(Soft again, laughter and tears in it)

Doesn't friendship grow to that? To love?
Doesn't forty years amount to anything?
We've cast our lot together, boy, we're
friends, we've been through lots of thick
OR thin together. Which is it, boy?

(Shout)

WHICH IS IT, BOY?! THICK?! THIN?!
WELL, WHATEVER IT IS, WE'VE BEEN
THROUGH IT, BOY!

(Soft)

And you don't have to ask. I like you,
Harry, yes, I really do, I don't like Edna,
but that's not half the point, I like you
fine; I find my liking you has limits. . . .

(Loud)

BUT THOSE ARE MY LIMITS! NOT
YOURS!

(Soft)

The fact I like you well enough, but not enough . . . that best friend in the world should be something else—more—well, that's my poverty. So, bring your wife, and bring your terror, bring your plague.

(Loud)

BRING YOUR PLAGUE!

(The four women appear in the archway, coffee cups in hand, stand, watch)

I DON'T WANT YOU HERE!
YOU ASKED?!
NO! I DON'T

(Loud)

BUT BY CHRIST YOU'RE GOING TO STAY HERE! YOU'VE GOT THE RIGHT! THE RIGHT! DO YOU KNOW THE WORD? THE RIGHT!

(Soft)

You've put nearly forty years in it, baby; so have I, and if it's nothing, I don't give a damn, you've got the right to be here, you've earned it

(Loud)

AND BY GOD YOU'RE GOING TO TAKE IT! DO YOU HEAR ME?! YOU BRING YOUR TERROR AND YOU COME IN HERE AND YOU LIVE WITH US! YOU BRING YOUR PLAGUE! YOU STAY WITH US! I DON'T WANT YOU HERE! I DON'T LOVE YOU! BUT BY GOD . . . YOU STAY!!

(Pause)

STAY!

(Softer)

Stay!

(Soft, tears)

Stay. Please? Stay?

(Pause)

Stay? Please? Stay?

(A silence in the room. HARRY, *numb, rises; the women come into the room, slowly, stand. The play is quiet and subdued from now until the end)*

EDNA *(Calm)*

Harry, will you bring our bags down? Maybe Tobias will help you. Will you ask him?

HARRY *(Gentle)*

Sure.

(Goes to TOBIAS, *who is quietly wiping tears from his face, takes him gently by the shoulder)*

Tobias? Will you help me? Get the bags upstairs? (TOBIAS *nods, puts his arm around* HARRY. *The two men exit. Silence)*

EDNA

(Stirring her coffee; slightly strained, but conversational)

Poor Harry; he's not a . . . callous man, for all his bluff.

(Relaxing a little, almost a contentment)

He . . . he came to my bed last night, got in with me, I . . . let him stay, and talk. I let him think I . . . wanted to make love; he . . . it pleases him, I think—to know he would be wanted, if he . . . He said to me . . . He . . . he lay there in the dark with me—this man—and he said to me, very softly, and like a little boy, rather: "Do they love us? Do they love us, Edna?" Oh, I let a silence go by. "Well . . . as much as we love them . . . I should think."

(Pause)

The hair on his chest is very gray . . . and soft. "Would . . . would we let them stay, Edna?" Almost a whisper. Then still again.

(Kindly)

Well, I hope he told Tobias something simple, something to help. We mustn't press our luck, must we: test.

(Pause. Slight smile)

It's sad to come to the end of it, isn't it, nearly the end; so much more of it gone by . . . than left, and still not know—still not have learned . . . the boundaries, what we may not do . . . not ask, for fear of looking in a mirror. We *shouldn't* have come.

AGNES *(A bit by rote)*

Now, Edna . . .

EDNA

For our own sake; our own . . . lack. It's sad to know you've gone through it all, or most of it, without . . . that the one body you've wrapped your arms around . . . the only skin you've ever known . . . is your own—and that it's dry . . . and not warm.

(Pause. Back to slightly strained conversational tone)

What will you do, Julia? Will you be seeing Douglas?

JULIA *(Looking at her coffee)*

I haven't thought about it; I don't know; I doubt it.

AGNES

Time.

(Pause. They look at her)

Time happens, I suppose.

(Pause. They still look)

To people. Everything becomes . . . too late, finally. You know it's going on . . . up on the hill; you can see the dust, and hear the cries, and the steel . . . but you wait; and time happens. When you *do* go, sword, shield . . . finally . . . there's nothing there . . . save rust; bones; and the wind.

(Pause)

I'm sorry about the coffee, Edna. The help must hide the beans, or take them with them when they go to bed.

EDNA

Oooh. Coffee and wine: they're much the same with me—I can't tell good from bad.

CLAIRE

Would anyone . . . besides Claire . . . care to have a drink?

AGNES *(Muttered)*

Oh, really, Claire.

CLAIRE

Edna?

EDNA *(Little deprecating laugh)*

Oh, good heavens, thank you, Claire. No.

CLAIRE

Julia?

JULIA

(Looks up at her; steadily; slowly)
All right; thank you. I will.

EDNA

(As AGNES *is about to speak; rising)*
I think I hear the men.
*(*TOBIAS *and* HARRY *appear in the archway, with bags)*

TOBIAS

We'll just take them to the car, now.
(They do so)

EDNA

(Pleasant, but a little strained)
Thank you, Agnes, you've been . . . well, just thank you. We'll be seeing
you.

AGNES

(Rises, too; some worry on her face)
Yes; well, don't be strangers.

EDNA *(Laughs)*
Oh, good Lord, how could we be? Our lives are . . . the same.
(Pause)
Julia . . . think a little.

JULIA *(A trifle defiant)*
Oh, I will, Edna. I'm fond of marriage.

EDNA

Claire, my darling, *do* be good.

CLAIRE

(Two drinks in her hands; bravura)
Well, I'll try to be quiet.

EDNA

I'm going into town on Thursday, Agnes. Would you like to come?
(A longer pause than necessary, CLAIRE *and* JULIA *look at* AGNES*)*

AGNES *(Just a trifle awkward)*
Well . . . no, I don't think so, Edna; I've . . . I've so much to do.

EDNA *(Cooler; sad)*

Oh. Well . . . perhaps another week.

AGNES

Oh, yes; we'll do it.
(The men reappear)

TOBIAS

(Somewhat formal, reserved)
All done.

HARRY *(Slight sigh)*

All set.

AGNES

(Going to HARRY, *embracing him)*
Harry, my darling; take good care.

HARRY

(Kisses her, awkwardly, on the cheek)
Th-thank you, Agnes; you, too, Julia? You . . . you be good.

JULIA

Goodbye, Harry.

CLAIRE *(Handing* JULIA *her drink)*
'Bye, Harry: see you 'round.

HARRY *(Smiles, a little ruefully)*

Sure thing, Claire.

EDNA *(Embraces* TOBIAS*)*
Goodbye, Tobias . . . thank you.

TOBIAS *(Mumbled)*

Goodbye, Edna.
(Tiny silence)

HARRY

(Puts his hand out, grabs TOBIAS', *shakes it hard)*
Thanks, old man.

TOBIAS *(Softly; sadly)*

Please? Stay?
(Pause)

HARRY *(Nods)*

See you at the club. Well? Edna?

(They start out)

AGNES *(After them)*

Drive carefully, now. It's Sunday.

EDNA'S AND HARRY'S VOICES

All right. Goodbye. Thank you.

(The four in the room together. JULIA *and* CLAIRE *have sat down;* AGNES *moves to* TOBIAS, *puts her arm around him)*

AGNES *(Sigh)*

Well. Here we all are. You all right, my darling?

TOBIAS *(Clears his throat)*

Sure.

AGNES

(Still with her arm around him)

Your daughter has taken to drinking in the morning, I hope you'll notice.

TOBIAS *(Unconcerned)*

Oh?

(Moves away from her)

I had one here . . . somewhere, one with Harry. Oh, there it is.

AGNES

Well, I would seem to have *three* early-morning drinkers now. I hope it won't become a club. We'd have to get a license, would we not?

TOBIAS

Just think of it as very late at night.

AGNES

All right, I will.

(Silence)

TOBIAS

I tried.

(Pause)

I was honest.

(Silence)

Didn't I?

(Pause)

Wasn't I?

JULIA *(Pause)*

You were very honest, Father. And you tried.

TOBIAS

Didn't I try, Claire? Wasn't I honest?

CLAIRE *(Comfort; rue)*

Sure you were. You tried.

TOBIAS

I'm sorry. I apologize.

AGNES *(To fill a silence)*

What I find most astonishing—aside from my belief that I will, one day
. . . lose my mind—but when? Never, I begin to think, as the years go by,
or that I'll not *know* if it happens, or maybe even *has*—what I find most
astonishing, I think, is the wonder of daylight, of the sun. All the centuries, millenniums—all the history—I wonder if that's why we sleep at
night, because the darkness still . . . frightens us? They say we sleep to
let the demons out—to let the mind go raving mad, our dreams and
nightmares all our logic gone awry, the dark side of our reason. And
when the daylight comes again . . . comes order with it.

(Sad chuckle)

Poor Edna and Harry.

(Sigh)

Well, they're safely gone . . . and we'll all forget . . . quite soon.

(Pause)

Come now; we can begin the day.

CURTAIN